Africa today

The rapidly increasing importance of Africa in world affairs is now only too apparent, but the picture it presents today in the media is one of great complexity, confusion and even impending disaster. It is very easy to take refuge in simplistic, over-generalized and highly prejudiced explanations of its current problems, blaming colonial exploitation, neocolonialism, international capitalism, communism, tribalism, élitism, corruption or even simple ineptness for the present state of social, economic and political disorder in Africa. The aim of this short, readable and authoritative book is to provide an introduction to the understanding of events in Africa today, and to stimulate an informed interest in the very difficult and complex problems with which African governments are now having to grapple.

B. W. HODDER *is Professor of Geography in the University of London.*

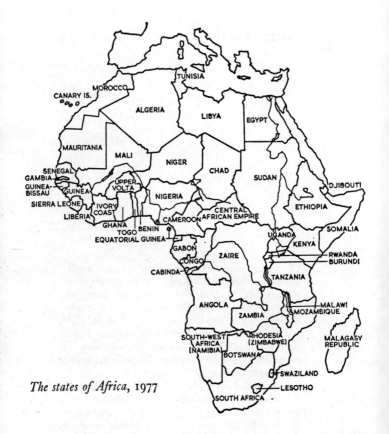

The states of Africa, 1977

B. W. HODDER

Africa
today

*a short introduction
to African affairs*

AFRICANA PUBLISHING
COMPANY NEW YORK
A division of Holmes & Meier Publishers, Inc.

First published in the United States of America 1978 *by*
AFRICANA PUBLISHING COMPANY
A division of Holmes & Meier Publishers, Inc.
30 *Irving Place, New York,* N.Y. 10003
Copyright © 1978 *by B. W. Hodder*

Library of Congress Cataloging in Publication Data

Hodder, B. W.
   Africa today.

   Bibliography: p.
   Includes index.
   1. Africa—Politics and government—1960–
I. Title.
DT30.H55 1978   320.9′6′03   78–8218
ISBN 0–8419–0395–6

ISBN 0–8419–0404–9 (*Paperback*)

PRINTED IN GREAT BRITAIN

To Ian, Greg, Jean,
Tamsin and Rupert

Contents

Preface

The aim of this short book is to provide an introduction to the understanding of African affairs today. Emphasis is placed on certain major issues facing independent African states and attracting increasing attention and concern in the world at large. It might reasonably be argued that in choosing to cover such a broad spectrum of issues in such a brief compass I have set myself an impossible task. Admittedly it has been difficult to avoid over-simplifications and doubtful generalizations; and many will disagree with some of the interpretations, viewpoints and judgements. Yet in talking to a wide range of audiences over the past few years I have found a real need for a simply written book of this kind – not primarily factual in content, but designed to stimulate an informed interest in the very difficult and complex problems with which African governments are now having to grapple.

London, 1977   B.W.H.

Introduction

It is now only too apparent that Africa will occupy an increasingly important place in international affairs in the foreseeable future. But the picture Africa presents today in the media is one of great complexity, confusion and, perhaps, impending disaster. Faced with such a picture, however inaccurate, the general reader can perhaps be forgiven for taking a pessimistic, despairing and essentially negative view of Africa and its future. Moreover, it is only too easy to take refuge in simplistic, over-generalized and highly prejudiced explanations of current problems, blaming colonial exploitation, neo-colonialism, international capitalism, communism, ethnicity, corruption or even simple ineptness for the present state of social, economic and political disorder in Africa. How far is such pessimism justified? And how many, if any, of these broad generalizations are valid?

It seems sensible to begin by making a number of general

but necessary remarks about this vast continent. Among the chief causes of the recent upsurge of interest in African affairs has been the unprecedented speed and scale of political change in the continent. With few exceptions, the post-war race to independence began in the late 1950s, reached a climax in the 1960–2 period, by which time over twenty independent African nations had emerged, and has now nearly run its course with the rapid withdrawal of Portugal from her southern African territories (see the map on p. ii).

For many observers the term 'independent' is unacceptable, since it can be argued that gaining independence from a former colonial power has been shown to be no guarantee at all of true political, social or economic independence. But the same could be said of many if not most other countries in the world, including developed countries; and in this sense African countries have as much right to be called independent as does any other similarly large group of states. Many of these new African nations are small, and taken individually they might seem to have, at first sight, very little demographic, economic or political significance, let alone viability. But taken together – and this is really the point here – the independent African states today form a politically powerful group, representing nearly one-third of the total voting strength of the United Nations General Assembly. Furthermore, the success or failure of African governments in dealing with a wide range of social, political and economic problems will have implications reaching far beyond the shores of Africa. Problems of national cohesion and stability; the legitimacy of state boundaries, especially, perhaps, for the fourteen landlocked states; the most appropriate form of government; ethnicity; élitism; the ideological conflict between the western and communist worlds; the continued existence of white minority governments; the prospects for regional cooperation in Africa; the need for a sound and prosperous economic base; and African unity: these are some of the many critical issues with which independent African governments are now faced.

Only the most ingenuous observer would suggest that the way in which these complex and often intractable problems

2

are tackled is of concern only to Africans. It is possible, for instance, that apartheid and white minority regimes in southern Africa could lead to a major racial conflict with worldwide repercussions. Interest in Africa today is also part of a general concern with the 'developing' or 'third' world, of which all African countries except South Africa are members. Many writers accept that economic development in these countries is the responsibility not only of African governments but also of the peoples of the developed world; for only with external capital, technical aid and new trading opportunities, so the argument goes, can the economies of African countries reasonably be expected to prosper. On the other hand, other writers argue that it is precisely this continuing dependency of African countries on the developed industrial world that is responsible for the chronic state of underdevelopment in the continent.

Africa's variety

To make any useful generalizations about Africa is not an easy task, for variety, complexity, the exception to the rule – these are the keynotes of African affairs. And yet one of the commonest generalizations made about Africa is that it is a continent markedly lacking in variety.

There are three main reasons why this statement is so often made. First, European knowledge of this vast continent is both recent and slight. Many of the simplest geographical facts about Africa, especially to the south of the Sahara, were not known to Europeans until well into the nineteenth century; and systematic scientific and historical investigation is, for most of Africa, strictly a twentieth-century phenomenon. Secondly, the sheer size of Africa – over 11,500,000 square miles and so the largest continent after Asia – is not easily appreciated and is responsible for much current misunderstanding about African life and environments. A simple but significant difference between Africa and Europe, for instance, is that the units of comparison are so very much larger in Africa. The Sahara, the tropical rainforests, the high plains and

3

plateaux, the rift-valley systems of eastern Africa, the Niger, Chad, Zaïre (Congo) and Zambezi basins, the Nile valley: all these refer to physical units vastly larger than anything to be found in Europe. Finally, Africa is a strikingly compact continent. It has very few coastal indentations and, with a coastline of only 16,000 miles or so, readily gives the impression of being smaller and more uniform than it really is.

If, then, Africa is characterized by variety rather than uniformity, in what particular ways does this variety express itself? And how does this affect the kinds of issues with which we are here primarily concerned? One important way in which this occurs is reflected in the very complex pattern of colonial associations. Take, for instance, Senegal, Kenya and Angola. Their official languages, administrative institutions, educational systems, architecture, the very crops they grow – all these reflect clearly the colonial associations, respectively French, British and Portuguese, of these three contrasting states. Variety is also expressed in the complex ideological pattern which has followed on from or has developed as a reaction to the colonial experience. Compare, for example, the socialist idealism of Tanzania with the western capitalist materialism of countries like the Ivory Coast or South Africa. Whilst admittedly a significant majority of Africans are as yet little politicized, it remains true that these widely contrasting ideologies deeply affect the entire social, economic and political fabric of African states, determining, among other things, the purpose and ends of state activity. Then again, Africa is politically the most fragmented of all the continents, for only in Europe, Central America and the Caribbean is there anything approaching Africa's patchwork-quilt of states. Divided into some fifty political units, Africa already commands a much more powerful voice in world affairs than her relatively small population of rather over 400,000,000 would otherwise suggest.

Africa is also exceptionally varied physically. Admittedly, most of Africa is remarkable for the level and undisturbed nature of its ancient surfaces, which cover more than a third of the continent: in the centre and west they form extensive

4

plateaux at some 2,000 feet, while in the east and south the high plateaux average some 4,000 feet above sea level. But although these huge expanses are characteristic features of the African landscape, they are interrupted by steeply folded and sharply eroded mountain ranges in the northern and southern extremities of the continent, by mountain massifs in the Sahara and parts of East Africa, by the complex rift-valley systems of north-eastern and eastern Africa, and by local volcanic features like the Cameroon Mountains of western Africa. In its climate and vegetation Africa ranges from hot deserts to equatorial rainforests, from Mediterranean woodland and scrub to the whole complex of tropical savannas. Soils vary widely, often over very short distances, and include a variety of leached soils, together with the richer brown earths, alluvials and many different types of volcanic soils. Furthermore, African mainland states vary in size from under 1,000 square miles to almost 1,000,000 square miles; Sudan, the largest, is about three-quarters the size of India. The states of Africa also include largely forest states like Gabon, savanna states like Tanzania, desert states like Mauritania, and almost entirely mountainous countries like Lesotho.

Then, of course, great diversity characterizes Africa's population. Densities vary dramatically, but the average density for the continent as a whole is less than half the world average and the second lowest of any inhabited continent (see the table on pp. 155–6). Although Africa comprises about 22 per cent of the world's land surface (excluding Antarctica) it contains barely 10 per cent of the world's peoples. Some writers argue that this low density has quite fundamental social, political and economic implications, mostly working to Africa's disadvantage. On the other hand, there are certain limited areas of high population density, notably along the coast of the Atlas lands of North Africa, the lower Nile valley, sections of West Africa, discontinuous areas in the lakes region of East Africa, and parts of South Africa.

Considered by countries, the most populous African state is Nigeria with some 76,000,000 people, or almost a fifth of the total population in Africa. A few countries have populations

5

of between 10,000,000 and 20,000,000, but most African states contain under 5,000,000 inhabitants, and no less than 13 have under 2,000,000 each. The population base of many African countries, then, is small, with important implications for their future economic and political independence. This is especially true of those countries whose small populations are contained in large territorial areas: Mauritania, Mali, Niger, Chad, much of Sudan and Botswana are examples of countries where grave economic and administrative problems arise from such conditions.

Another way in which the variety of Africa's population is expressed is in its urban/rural composition. Africa is the least urbanized of the inhabited continents, there being in 1976 only 150 or so towns with populations of over 100,000. With the exception of South Africa and Egypt the rural population percentage of all countries exceeds 60 per cent. Towns are nevertheless of particular importance in any study of contemporary Africa for the simple reason that many current social, economic and political changes are focused there. This remains true even though the towns are usually not very large, less than 20 having populations of over 500,000. Much of the urban settlement in Africa, moreover, is of European origin. Only in the Muslim lands along the Mediterranean coast and in parts of West Africa is there any widespread indigenous urban tradition. Cities of European origin, like Nairobi in Kenya, contrast markedly with indigenous cities like Ibadan in Nigeria.

But above all, perhaps, the population of Africa is strikingly varied in its ethnic composition. The African peoples are at least as varied as the indigenous peoples of any other continent. However one classifies them, the pattern is immensely complex. There are many hundreds of ethnic groups, language groups and religions. The peoples of Africa, too, are of many physical types, at many different levels of economic, social and political development, and they have reacted in differing ways to the impact of European colonial rule. Just as there is really no such thing as a typical 'African landscape', so there is no such person as a typical 'African'.

6

Furthermore, the diverse pattern of African ethnic and linguistic groups is immensely complicated by international migrations, as well as by the infusion of European and Asian minorities. There are some 5,000,000 Europeans or those of European stock in southern Africa. There are also Europeans, as well as Americans, Australians and Canadians, in most of the larger towns outside southern Africa, and a still wider scattering of European traders, missionaries, miners, officials, advisers and technicians, including many now working for independent African governments. In some parts of Africa, too, Chinese, Cubans and Russians comprise small but often highly significant minorities. Then the ethnic pattern is further complicated by Indian minorities in eastern Africa who fulfil, or in some cases used to fulfil, an important economic role; and they form an even more significant minority in South Africa. They are mainly shopkeepers and traders who live in the cities and are sometimes subjected to a good deal of discrimination. There is also a considerable Arab element in the population of Africa. In addition to the Arab-speaking and Islamized majorities in all the countries of North Africa, which derive from the Muslim conquests of the seventh and later centuries AD, Arabs comprise a distinctive minority along the east coast, notably in Kenya and Tanzania, where some settled as far back as 1,500 years ago. Over the centuries, and with the spread of Islam, pilgrimage routes reinforced trade links.

Finally, the racial composition of the population of Africa is complicated by the existence of people of mixed blood. The Coloureds of South Africa and the *mistos* of Angola and Mozambique are largely the product of Europeans mixing with African peoples, but they include also Hottentot survivors and other minor elements, such as the Cape Malays who stem from Indonesian slaves imported by the Dutch in the seventeenth and eighteenth centuries.

The variety of Africa, then, is a fact of great and underlying importance; and each state reflects this variety in often strikingly different ways. Yet to exaggerate this variety is both wrong and pointless, more especially as many social and

7

political arguments postulate the existence of some sense of 'being an African' and because a good deal of economic thinking is directed at regional economic cooperation between groupings of states. It is perhaps useful to distinguish six rather conventional regional groups of states in Africa: North Africa, North-East Africa, East Africa, West Africa, Equatorial and Central Africa, and Southern Africa (see the table on pp. 155–6).

The two Africas

Grouping states together in this way, however, obscures that simplest of all divisions in Africa – the great geographical dichotomy between Africa lying to the north and south of the Sahara. Historically, as well as physically, Africa north of the Sahara has a closer affinity with Mediterranean Europe than with the rest of Africa. Extensions of Phoenician, Greek, Roman and Muslim civilizations flowered there in northern Africa, which provides a unique and rich field for the study of culture contact and succession. South of the Sahara, however, relatively little is as yet known of its early history. Contacts across the Sahara were not lacking. In the moister climate of the fourth millennium BC there were significant contacts across the Sahara, and much of the archaeological and artistic evidence now available indicates how important and strong these trans-Saharan contacts must have been. More recently, and certainly after the eighth century AD, by which time the camel had been introduced into northern Africa, substantial trading contacts developed between the Mediterranean coast and the southern fringes of the Sahara desert – the savanna belt stretching right across the continent from the Atlantic in the west to the upper Nile in the east; and in these savanna lands arose subsequently a succession of often powerful indigenous states whose very life lay in their ability to trade across the Sahara with the Mediterranean world.

Contacts with sub-Saharan Africa were also made up the Nile valley, from Arabia across to Ethiopia and Somalia, and by Arabs who reached the east coast of Africa in their *dhows* at least as early as the tenth century AD. Our knowledge of all these early states and contacts south of the Sahara is as yet fragmentary, but it is already quite sufficient to refute the suggestion that Africa south of the Sahara 'has no history'. Archaeological and serological research, as well as the use of Arabic and traditional, including oral, sources in the writing of African history by African scholars, has begun to open up vast and exciting new perspectives. Apart from the ancient savanna or sudanic states already referred to – such as Ghana, Mali, Mossi, Songhai, Hausa, Bornu, Kanem, Wadai, Darfur and the Funj Sultanate – core areas of ancient African states existed elsewhere, as in Buganda, Kongo, Merina (Malagasy) and Zimbabwe (Rhodesia). Many of these early civilizations are now known to have been both extensive and advanced. It was only to European eyes that the continent to the south of the Sahara appeared a dark, mysterious and above all primitive world – the Dark Continent – until after the first Portuguese voyages along the coast in the fifteenth century. Indeed much of the African interior remained unknown to Europeans until the last quarter of the nineteenth century.

We are now in a position to ask ourselves a quite fundamental question, and the answer we give will affect very much our attitude to the analysis and understanding of African affairs today. Why, in spite of the continent's relative proximity to Europe, was Africa south of the Sahara so late in being opened up to European knowledge and influence? Answers to this question sometimes appeal to the deterrent effects of the physical environment: penetration inland was discouraged by the lack of many large and deep coastal embayments, and by the fact that some of the plateaux of Africa extend right up to the coast and result in falls on the lower courses of the rivers and in silting at the river mouths. Penetration inland was also made hazardous by the high incidence of disease. Landing on the coast itself was usually difficult because of the dangerous surf and steep sandy beaches, mangrove swamps or coral. Strong coastal currents frequently discouraged contact by sea. In West Africa, for instance, the early travel accounts make frequent mention of the problem known as 'getting off the coast', for vessels rounding the West African bulge were swept eastwards and in towards the coast by the eastward-setting currents and south-westerly winds. There is also the simple but powerful fact of the Sahara, that great stretch of desert extending right up to the west coast of Africa and covering about a quarter of the continent's area. At least for the last 2,000 or 3,000 years this must have acted as a deterrent to movement and contact between peoples. Even the Nile routes southwards through the desert end up in the *sudd* swamps of southern Sudan or in the fastnesses of the Ethiopian highlands.

There is little doubt that all these physical factors helped delay European contact and penetration in Africa south of the Sahara. But their significance can be exaggerated. According to Herskovits, over-emphasis on the physical constraints and limitations has been largely responsible 'for the fiction of Africa that for centuries lay dormant, out of contact with the rest of the world, impervious to impulses emanating from centres of civilization'.[1] It is pointed out that other largely tropical and even more distant areas, notably in Central America and the East Indies, had similar if not worse physical difficulties for Europeans to cope with. Other non-physical reasons must therefore be sought to account satisfactorily for the relatively late penetration by Europeans into Africa south of the Sahara.

Prominent among these was the lack of any strong motive for European involvement. Until well into the slaving era, especially in the eighteenth and early nineteenth centuries, European overseas commerce concentrated on the Far Eastern trade; and many of the first European coastal settlements in Africa, including those at the Cape of Good Hope, were related to this overriding interest in the Far East. Furthermore, even when slave trading in Africa became substantial, Europeans had little incentive for penetrating inland. Indigenous Africans or middlemen at or near the coast were only too ready to act for European slave traders but were less willing to allow any direct penetration inland by Europeans. As Oliver and Fage have put it, 'most of the African peoples, moreover, were organized into states and communities powerful enough to deter invaders and migrants from overseas until late in the nineteenth century . . . it was in large measure the progress made by Africans in earlier centuries that enabled them to resist the modern age for so long'.[2] It is relevant, too, that most African peoples have always been continental rather than maritime in their interests: to some groups – for example the Yoruba – the sea was indeed fetish. Not until the second half of the nineteenth century did any substantial opening-up of sub-Saharan Africa to European contact begin. It is true that the Portuguese 'discovered' much of the coast after the middle of the fifteenth century and even penetrated up part of the Zambezi valley in the early part of the sixteenth century; there was also considerable Dutch settlement at the Cape from the middle of the seventeenth century. But none of these contacts led immediately to any large-scale penetration of the interior.

The scramble for Africa

Until well into the nineteenth century, then, European settlements were for the most part restricted to small coastal trading stations. But during the nineteenth century European explorers began to make significant advances into tropical Africa. First among these included Mungo Park, Clapperton and Lander – all in West Africa – and during the middle years of the nineteenth century exploration extended farther inland and included the great trans-Saharan and sudanic journeys of Barth. Meanwhile, between 1841 and 1863 Livingstone, Burton, Speke and Grant increased Europe's knowledge of and interest in the east and south-east of the continent; and in the 1870s Stanley completed his famous trans-continental journey and other travels in Central Africa. It was in fact Livingstone's explorations in the east of the Congo basin, and Stanley's first epic journey across Africa from Zanzibar to the mouth of the Congo in 1874, that really opened up the Congo to European influence – an influence which, it was hoped, would open a path for commerce and Christianity and destroy the evils of African tribal society and the Arab slave trade. As a result of these and numerous other explorations and journeys, too, many of the great puzzles of African geography for Europeans – notably the courses of the Nile, Niger, Congo (Zaïre) and Zambezi rivers – were solved within the space of half a century. By the 1880s the main drainage and relief features of the continent were beginning to be mapped more or less accurately. During the same period missionaries took an increasing part in extending European interests.

All this exploration and evangelism frequently led to trade. Yet it was soon realized that profitable trade depended on the maintenance of peace and that this peace could not be assured without administrative intervention and control in the hinterlands. Because the explorers, missionaries, traders and administrators came from several different European countries – Spain, Portugal, France, Britain, Belgium and Germany – Africa soon became a field for the conflicting ambitions of the major European colonial powers. By the early 1880s these conflicting ambitions were beginning to be expressed territorially. Sections of the coast were being claimed by traders and administrators of one or other European power. Missionary, trading, military and administrative activities were beginning to expand inland from some of the coastal footholds. The stage was now set for the European scramble for Africa, finally to be set in motion by the 1884–5 Conference and Treaty of Berlin. This laid down that European colonial claims to territory could only be secured by what was termed 'effective occupation'; in other words European powers with interests on the African coast had to move inland to secure their hinterlands. The subsequent scramble for territory by European powers took place so rapidly that within a decade or so the broad outlines of most of the colonial territories – and, significantly, of most of the present independent African states – were laid down.

1 The colonial impact
and independence

The colonial impact

The extent and effects of the European colonial impact have been described by many writers. According to Perham,

> until the very recent penetration by Europe, the greater part of Africa was without the wheel, was without the plough and transport animals. It was without writing and so without history. Mentally and physically the African was helpless before a European intrusion all the more speedy and overwhelming because it came at a time when science had given Europe such tremendous material power.[3]

Such a view is now thought by African scholars to be somewhat extreme, ignoring as it does the new perspectives on history referred to earlier. Nevertheless some authors compare the social changes that took place in Africa during the colonial period with those that occurred in Western Europe when peasants and craftsmen were replaced by agricultural labourers and factory workers. In Africa, however, it is recognized that these changes were both more sudden and of external, colonial, origin. They arose from the unrestrained impact of European civilization upon African societies, and from the resultant contacts between widely disparate levels of technical advancement, methods of administrative organization and codes of conduct.

Yet while it is beyond question that many of the problems now facing African nations can be traced back to the colonial period, it is equally true that many of the root causes lie much further back in pre-colonial African societies and cultures. Africa's history is marked by great length and continuity. The colonial period was but a brief episode in the long history of Africa, producing what is in some senses no more than a veneer over the solid base of African life and culture. Certainly the colonial impact was initially rather slight. Conscious attempts at social, economic and political developments were the exception rather than the rule for some thirty to forty years after partition. This impact also took place upon societies in Africa which were neither static nor homogeneous; not only were there differing colonial policies and attitudes, but there were many different types of societies, economies and political systems within which colonial action took place. There was a confused, complex and fluid picture, rather than a simple impact of European control upon a uniformly passive, static or 'backward' African society. Africans, indeed, have always been highly selective in their acceptance of European ideas and techniques, and some societies have been much more receptive to change than others. Thus while it is legitimate for our general purposes here to isolate the European impact, it has to be recognized that this could operate only within the dynamic context of ethnicity and indigenous polities, economies and societies. Many European administrators soon realized that they could not afford to ignore existing local societies in formulating policies. As Lugard put it, 'the attempt to bridge the centuries without adequate study of other mentalities, traditions and beliefs is more likely to lead to failure than to success'.[4]

14

Nevertheless, the colonial impact has affected in a number of ways the particular issues which concern us here. The comparative study of colonial policies in Africa is a matter of some importance, for Africa was the most completely colonized of all the continents and most African states owe their territorial identity to their different colonial histories. With the exception of Liberia, all countries in Africa have experienced in some way and to some degree one or more periods of European colonial rule, even Ethiopia being for a few years under Italian rule. An understanding of the principal differences between the different colonial policies is therefore crucial. It is true that both Britain and France nurtured grand designs in Africa – the French ambition of French Africa stretching from the Mediterranean down to the Congo (Zaïre), and the British desire to 'paint the map red' from Cairo to the Cape. But in spite of this there were many important contrasts in their colonial policies.

Of all forms of colonialism in Africa the British is perhaps the most difficult to generalize about because it refers to such large and diverse areas of the continent, and because the British approach to colonial administration was essentially pragmatic and decentralized. Through the policy of what was known as 'indirect rule' Britain maintained the indigenous cultures and societies by working wherever possible through local social and political systems. Control was maintained – at least in theory – without any undue taking-over of power. In spite of all its limitations, indirect rule proved to be an economical system in that it allowed large areas to be administered by relatively few officials. But because it depended on the strength and coherence of traditional ethnic societies, its effectiveness was very much reduced in those areas where local indigenous institutions were weak. Moreover, in certain areas, as in Kenya and southern Africa, European settlement was an important consideration in formulating and carrying out policy, whereas in West Africa there was no substantial white settlement, and this difference resulted in important regional variations in colonial practice. And when Britain became committed to encouraging evolution from colonial to commonwealth or independent status for all its African territories, this proved to be a much easier task in those areas where white settlement was small or negligible than where there were substantial numbers of European settlers – above all, of course, in Rhodesia and South Africa. Nevertheless, Britain was responsible for establishing peace and security, including the setting up of effective local police forces, and there was substantial British investment in most of her African colonies.

Unlike British colonial policy, that of the French was for long committed to the idea of assimilation rather than to eventual independence: her territories in Africa were not so much French colonies as simply part of Overseas France. French colonial administration was therefore more direct and centralized than its British counterpart. French policy depended upon relatively large numbers of French administrators and generally did not attempt to work through existing local social or political institutions. Little encouragement was given to local cultures or languages. Emphasis in French Africa was on the creation of a small African élite, very often educated in France; there was little in the way of a colour bar, Frenchmen being found in some of the more lowly occupations and Africans in some of the more senior ones. White settlement was numerically important only in North Africa, but significant minorities were to be found in Dakar (Senegal) and in the plantation areas of Guinea, the Ivory Coast, Cameroon and Madagascar. During the years following 1945, however, France moved by stages from a policy of assimilation to a policy of association; and even this was subsequently abandoned, although it remained an important inspiration in French policy.

Belgian control was confined to one large territory – the Belgian Congo – in the heart of the continent. The Belgian Congo began as the personal possession of King Leopold. Like that of the French, Belgian policy was highly centralized – in this case effectively in Brussels – but, like that of the British, it was aimed at eventual independence. Belgian policy was also essentially long-term and theoretical. It was argued that for many years careful tuition would be necessary before

Africans could properly assume control in the Congo. Priority was given to economic and social development: by first promoting social and economic betterment, the Belgians argued, 'we are forging the weapons with which the natives will conquer their political freedom, if we do not have the wisdom to grant it gracefully when the time is ripe'.[5] Educational policy was broadly based at the elementary level so that there was little growth of an African élite – at least an élite based on education, as in French and to some extent British Africa. It was firmly believed that literacy and broad-based economic and social foundations were necessary before political development could safely be encouraged. Indeed, political expression was denied to both Africans and Europeans until just before independence.

Of the other forms of European colonialism in Africa, that of the Portuguese is of particular interest today in that Portugal has suddenly withdrawn from its African territories. Like that of the French, Portuguese policy was aimed initially at assimilation, all territories being regarded as part of the Portuguese Union and, even with substantial numbers of white settlers, there was relatively little colour bar. The Spanish colonial system was similar to that of the Portuguese, but applied to small and what were then relatively unproductive territories in western Africa; the Western Sahara has now been divided between Mauritania and Morocco, and Spanish Guinea has become independent Equatorial Guinea. Spain now possesses only the presidio cities of Ceuta and Melilla in North Africa, and the Canary Islands. Finally, mention must be made of the German colonial period. Germany controlled considerable areas of Africa – Togo and Cameroon in West Africa, Tanganyika and Ruanda Urundi in East Africa, and South-West Africa – and, as far as it went, German colonial policy was akin to that of the French and emphasized economic development; but Germany's impact was limited in time by her defeat in the First World War. Her colonies were then mandated under the League of Nations and, later, under the United Nations Trusteeship Council, to other European powers – Britain, France and Belgium.

The various European powers, then, subjected most parts of the continent to their different forms of colonial rule. The three great European language groups of most significance today are English, French and Portuguese, and it is common to refer to Anglophone, Francophone and Lusophone Africa to cover their respective areas. Some writers suggest that the French were the most successful in that Francophone Africa demonstrates a greater degree of coherence. But the balance of opinion is probably that it would be misleading to suggest that there is any coherence between countries in each of these three groups; in sentiment, ideology or policy there is no significant common feature beyond the European language legacy.

Effects of colonialism

The underlying economic effects of Africa's colonial experience are impossible to ignore in any examination of African affairs today. Certainly the various colonial powers, following their own particular policies, often had very powerful economic effects, of which perhaps the most important from our point of view were to disrupt the predominantly subsistence economies and introduce Africans to a monetary exchange economy, more particularly by introducing and developing cash crops; to establish internal networks of transport and communications in the various territories; and to foster the growth of externally 'dependent' economies. Initially, it must be noted, the motivation for the European 'scramble' for Africa was certainly not primarily the need for tropical raw materials and foodstuffs in West European countries. While the prospects of economic gain undoubtedly provided a motive, in some cases a principal motive, it was not the only one. The concept of 'trusteeship' was frequently said to be, and in a few cases undoubtedly was, an important element in European interest in Africa. This is no mere rationalization. Any frank and unbiased reading of primary sources of the period makes it clear that some administrators did genuinely see themselves as having a duty to humanity to develop the vast human and material resources of this great continent. Furthermore, the ideal colony, particularly for the British, was not so much one that could provide raw materials as one that could be self-supporting financially, and this meant that taxes had to be paid and imposed, or at least that adequate customs dues had to be collected. This was impossible, however, before people had something to grow and sell, so that the problem was essentially one of creating opportunities to earn cash incomes which could then be taxed. Whichever way this was done – by peasant growing of cash crops, by plantations, or by mining – the incentive was the imposition of direct taxation. But cash incomes, and consequently taxation, could not be increased until governments had provided the necessary background of law and order by establishing the basic structure of civil administration.

Agriculture is still the most widespread activity in African countries, but it is now radically changed from what i t was before the colonial period of administration. Many agricultural land-use patterns are the direct result of European contacts. In southern West Africa, for instance, many of the food and cash crops grown today, with the notable exception of the indigenous oil palm, were introduced or developed by Europeans either before or during the colonial period. By the end of the colonial period agriculture in Africa comprised a wide range of different systems – from the temporary clearings of shifting cultivators to highly capitalized and mechanized plantations. Although by the end of the colonial period 60 per cent of Africa's agricultural land was still devoted primarily to subsistence farming, commercial crops (especially groundnuts, cotton, cocoa, coffee and oil palm) were by then being produced in modified local systems in Senegal, Ghana, Nigeria, Uganda and Ethiopia; and large-scale plantations characterized the production of palm products, rubber and cocoa in the Congo (Zaïre), sisal and tea in East Africa, and sugar in Angola and Uganda. European-owned companies and estates accounted for a high percentage of commercial agricultural output in Kenya, Rhodesia, South Africa, Algeria, Morocco and Tunisia.

Another important economic effect of European control was

the construction of new lines of transport. These were an important corollary of the new general peace of the colonial period, many of the earliest lines being built partly to facilitate control over the expanding hinterlands of the coastal protectorates or colonies, though this was bound up with the desire to facilitate internal and external trading and a general increase of production. In some areas, the use of rivers, lagoons and tidal creeks dominated the early pattern of transport. But in most cases rivers were found to be of poor value as commercial waterways, impeded as they so often are by shallows and rapids, and by sandbars across their mouths. Until the 1920s, roads were more often built or improved for military and strategic than for economic reasons, an attitude that was wholly understandable in that the chief means of moving all kinds of goods on land, at least in the forest zones, was by headloading; from the commercial point of view, therefore, it was only necessary to keep clear a path or track wide enough for a single file of head porters. By the time motor transport had become more common in the 1920s, however, one of the most powerful incentives for the building of motorable roads was the relatively high cost of head porterage and the difficulty of getting porters.

It was the railways, however, which perhaps best illustrated the European impact on transport. In West Africa the more developed, apparently more productive and certainly moister areas were to be found in the south near the coast, divided between several competing European powers. The British and French built railways inland from the coast, though the French, with their large contiguous areas in West Africa, planned their lines to link with and supplement the navigable sections of the Senegal and Niger rivers. The one common desire in all railway building in West Africa was to secure effective political control of the interior, and to develop and retain within a particular colony as much trade as possible. For Africa as a whole there were by the early 1960s nearly 30,000 miles of railways of different gauges, but relatively close networks existed only in the former French territories of North Africa and in South Africa, the latter possessing over a quarter of the total length of track in Africa. The most complete road systems were also in South Africa and the more populous parts of the Mediterranean littoral. On the other hand, the best waterways for navigation were in tropical Africa: the Congo (Zaïre) and its tributaries, the Senegal and Gambia, the Niger and Benue, the Great Lakes of East Africa, and the Nile. The economic infra-structure was gradually being built up by modernizing communications; road and rail networks were extended; waterways, coastal approaches and ports were improved; power potential, especially in hydro-electricity, was beginning to be developed; and most large cities in Africa were served by international air routes.

But perhaps the most significant economic legacy left by the colonial powers to African nations arises from the fact that the economies of the separate states are still very much the creation of the colonial countries which controlled them. Each of these economies is in some degree a dual economy – the indigenous, largely rural, subsistence economy; and the colonial, export-oriented economy, the latter being a classical economy with a limited range of products, limited capital and markets, and an emphasis on growing primary products or on mining for export. The economies of a majority of African countries, indeed, still depend on what has been called the colonial pattern of trade: their prosperity, such as it is, is excessively dependent on the export of a few primary products – mostly minerals and agricultural products such as copper, petroleum, cocoa, cotton, groundnuts and palm oil – and they are obliged to import most of the manufactured goods they need. Their economies are therefore subject to damaging fluctuations in world markets and prices for a very limited number of primary products, and there are few established overseas markets for such manufactured goods as they do produce.

As for the social and political effects of European control, we have already noted that the various colonial powers differed, often quite markedly, in their impact on African indigenous social and political systems; moreover, African societies themselves reacted in different ways to the European impact. Nevertheless, some generalizations are possible. Many of the effects of colonial contact were undoubtedly beneficial. In the field of health, whilst it is true that the Europeans sometimes introduced new diseases which decimated local populations, the general long-term effect of European rule was certainly to improve substantially general health standards and to reduce death rates. Europeans also affected the settlement geography of large parts of Africa, more particularly in the planning and establishing of urban centres. And however one might agree or disagree with particular colonial educational policies, there is no doubt that achievements in the field of education, by missionaries and by colonial governments, were considerable and, with the possible exception of the Belgian Congo, laid the basis for an indigenous professional and administrative nucleus in African countries. It is also true that Europeans established a general peace and the basic structure of law, order and administration within definite territorial limits. Added to this, specific systems of government, including those modelled on western systems of parliamentary democracy, were set up, common languages were introduced, and Africans were enabled to identify themselves as members of human groups much larger and, in the modern world, more viable than their small ethnic societies formerly allowed.

On the other hand, many writers now identify and emphasize the negative effects of European colonial rule in Africa. Attention is directed to the exploitation of Africa – of its wealth and its peoples – and to the disruptive and destructive effects Europeans had on indigenous social, political and economic institutions. The conscious purpose of the colonial involvement in Africa, so it is suggested, was to create and maintain dependency and underdevelopment, whether economic, social or political. Europeans have always been in Africa for what they could get out of it, and worked always from their implicit assumptions of technical, physical, mental and even moral superiority.

A good deal of contemporary comment on African affairs, then, reveals two often quite opposing assessments of the colonial period. One is that Europeans fulfilled a 'civilizing' mission in Africa: Europeans brought Africa out of the Dark

Ages and gave it a sound basis for future social, economic and political progress in the modern world – a basis which Africans are now, for the most part, intent on destroying. The contrary point of view is that most of Africa's problems today have their origin in the exploitative and destructive nature of European colonialism; that Europe created the dependency burden under which Africa now labours; and that Europe, to use Rodney's phrase, 'underdeveloped' Africa.[6] Perhaps both these viewpoints are a little extreme; and in any case the practical relevance of this question to African affairs today is surely only very slight. The colonial period, with all its benefits or ills, is now a fact of history. There is no point at all in examining what might or might not have happened in Africa had there been no European colonial experience. Independent African governments have for the most part accepted that they must now operate within the old colonial territorial boundaries and that they must face the objective realities of today rather than the subjective interpretations of their past. Nevertheless, it is true that the thoughts and attitudes of many Africans, especially African intellectuals, are still preoccupied with and are deeply affected by their recent colonial past; and this fact, with all its psychological and intellectual implications, is fundamental to any understanding of many of the issues with which subsequent chapters in this book are concerned.

Independence

The end of the colonial period in Africa was remarkable for two reasons. First, it took place with great speed. By the end of the Second World War in 1945 only Egypt, Ethiopia, Liberia and South Africa were independent. After the granting of independence to India in 1947 the early 1950s saw some progress towards independence in Africa: Libya in 1951, for instance. But to read the literature of the 1940s and early 1950s dealing with the move towards independence in Africa is a salutary experience, because almost without exception the writers of the day were pleading for time in which to prepare Africa for independence. In the mid-1940s several writers argued against any abrupt removal of the 'colonial yoke', calling for a gradual withdrawal within an unspecified but generous time limit. A few years later it was noted that Europeans had destroyed much of what was good or harmonious in African culture without being given the time to put anything stable or constructive in its place; it was suggested that the African would not be able to find his way through to true independence without further tutelage, and that he should not be left to his own devices. As late as 1955, Belgian authorities were still talking in terms of a thirty-year transitional period to independence for their Congo territory. But the floodgates were already opening. Sudan, Morocco and Tunisia became independent in 1956, Ghana in 1957, and Guinea in 1958. The peak decade of independence in Africa was undoubtedly 1960–70. Just as the decade 1885–95 saw the 'scramble for Africa', so the 1960–70 decade saw the 'scramble to get out of Africa'. In 1960 no fewer than fifteen states gained independence, and most African countries were independent by 1970, since when the remaining Portuguese and Spanish territories have achieved independence in one form or another. By late 1977 only South-West Africa (Namibia) and Rhodesia (Zimbabwe, which declared its independence illegally in 1965) remain mainland colonial territories as defined by the United Nations, though this is not to say that all African territories other than these two are now 'liberated', if only in the sense that they are free from direct colonial control.

Secondly, independence in Africa came about with very little preparation. It has already been noted that the different colonial governments saw eventual independence for their territories in different ways – the British and the Belgians envisaged complete independence at some future date, whereas for almost all the time the Portuguese and the French saw their African territories simply as part of the Portuguese Union or of Overseas France. Attitudes to preparation for independence were affected not only by these different colonial practices but also by different priorities in education and by different political philosophies. Then again, whereas eventual political independence was frequently accepted in principle, economic

24

independence was often implicitly rejected. Certainly as late as the 1950s there was remarkably little preparation in the colonial territories for true political and economic independence. And, as it turned out, all the European colonial powers were thinking and operating within far too generous time limits; they misread or ignored the realities of the political geography of post-war Africa; and they were clearly unaware of the forces for independence which were so soon to overwhelm them. On the other hand, it is perhaps wrong to attribute the onset of movements for independence solely or even largely to pressures from within Africa. Throughout the twentieth century, colonial powers were always chiefly concerned with non-African matters – with two World Wars and with the depression of the inter-war years. Just as the scramble to get into Africa was motivated by factors essentially European, so the scramble to get out of Africa was to some extent motivated by non-African factors. The effects of the Second World War, the increasing American influence in world politics, the change in international attitudes to colonialism: all these contributed to changes in colonial policy. In Africa, at least, it seems probable that the abandonment of empire resulted very largely from metropolitan change rather than from political change in the colonial territories themselves. Portugal's recent and rapid withdrawal from Africa provides clear support for such an analysis.

With only two decades or so at most of experience of self-government, African states are still suffering from this lack of preparation for the responsibilities which they so rapidly assumed. There has inevitably been much disillusionment. Independence has not always meant liberation, a reduction of dependency, or true political and economic independence. Nor has independence necessarily brought about social and economic progress or political stability. African states today are only too aware of the interdependence of political and economic progress; they are faced with an apparently endless range of intractable and quite basic problems – of economics, society and politics, whether national or international; and they are becoming increasingly aware of the dangers of neo-colonialism

25

or of a new imperialism in Africa. African nations have been forced to grapple with the problems and responsibilities as well as the opportunities of their colonial heritage. Their identities as nation states reflect their colonial past. Even their territorial boundaries are not African but European in origin; and it is to this question of boundaries that we now turn our attention.

2 African boundaries and landlocked states

Boundaries

Independence in Africa has so far resulted in very few boundary changes: the national boundaries of independent Africa are substantially the same as the political divisions of colonial Africa. And only in a few areas, notably in South Africa, are the boundaries significantly older than the late nineteenth century. Elsewhere, most state boundaries in Africa date from the period of the 'scramble for Africa'. Their peculiarities usually reflect rival claims and competing negotiations for treaties with local chiefs by European powers and chartered companies with commercial interests. Sometimes, however, boundaries reflect arbitrary personal decisions, one well-known example being the peculiar kink in the Kenyan-Tanzanian border. In 1886 the Anglo-German agreement on their respective zones of influence drew a line on the map from the mouth of the Umba river on the Indian Ocean to the parallel of one degree south on the eastern shore of Lake Victoria. If the line had been straight Mount Kilimanjaro would have been in the British zone. But Kaiser Frederick is said to have protested that this would give the British the two greatest mountains in Africa, the other being Mount Kenya. Queen Victoria thereupon gave Kilimanjaro to her son-in-law in the interests of family and international relations.

Once the colonial boundaries of Africa had been drawn up they acquired a permanence which, assisted by unified administrations within them, helped to engender modern African nationalism. The case of Gambia is perhaps the outstanding example in Africa of the permanence of a state whose boundaries defy any kind of logic. With an area of only some 4,000 square miles and a population of barely 500,000, Gambia extends for just over 200 miles along the Gambia river but nowhere reaches the natural margins of the river basin; nor does it reach the river's source, which lies in Guinea. Gambia, moreover, is never wider than 22 miles. The boundary between Gambia and Senegal cuts across natural features, ethnic groups and settlement patterns; it also largely isolates the southern region of Senegal (Casamance) from the rest of the country. The European colonial powers in this part of West Africa were fully aware of the arbitrary nature of the Gambian boundary, and French and British statesmen had long been agreed on the desirability of incorporating Gambia into its French-held hinterland, as well as on the compensation to be received by Britain. But, as Hargreaves has expressed it, Gambia, once created, 'clung to its precarious existence as if it were a living being and not an artificially contrived colony'.[7] Local interests – especially European commercial interests and those of the educated Africans – refused to countenance any change. The continued subjection of Gambia and Senegal to quite different colonial systems early created wide divergencies in administrative, cultural and economic patterns between the two countries; and this glaring example of political, economic and social incongruity has now been perpetuated in the contemporary pattern of independent states.

Despite all their imperfections, then, colonial boundaries have generally been accepted as the territorial frameworks for independence in Africa. However arbitrary these frameworks, they already existed on the ground and on maps at the time of independence and it was within their limits that African governments have had to operate. Moreover, the Organization of African Unity (OAU) adopted in 1963 a resolution to adhere to existing African boundaries.

Perhaps the main reason why there have been few border disputes so far is that most of the boundaries are only just beginning to mark the effective limits of national government: in some cases they still function as rather ill-defined frontier zones. Very many African states are divided by these incompletely controlled zones, across which much human movement takes place. Indeed the very concept of a formal boundary line is essentially of European colonial origin in much of Africa. The traditional concept in many parts of the continent – as, indeed, it was for long elsewhere in the world – was one of frontier marches: in North Africa, for instance, the geographical limits of the Muslim states were only vaguely circumscribed according to the allegiance of the people (*umma* or 'community of believers') to their spiritual rulers.

Today, however, the state and its boundaries everywhere provide the framework for nation-building throughout Africa and, as existing zones shrink to become lines of firm authority, it is likely that border disputes will increase in number and severity. There is already a good deal of evidence to support this prediction. The mid-1970s have witnessed a sudden and dramatic increase in boundary problems. The withdrawal of Spain from Western Sahara led to conflicting claims to the territory by Morocco and Mauritania, and to the eventual partition of the former colony, the northern two-thirds going to Morocco, the southern one-third to Mauritania. This arrangement, however, is opposed by Algeria and the north-eastern border of the former Spanish colony can still be said to be in a state of flux. In this case the dispute has both economic and strategic implications – the former colony has immensely rich resources of phosphates, and Algeria would clearly like to have access to the Atlantic seaboard. This whole issue is also bound up with the 'independence' question of the former Spanish

29

Sahara; the Polisario front is currently waging a guerrilla war against the 'occupying' powers of Morocco and Mauritania.

Another example of the recent intensification of boundary problems is in the Horn of Africa, where interest focuses on the territorial ambitions of Somalia. Somalia represents the fusion of two former colonial territories, British and Italian Somaliland. Her disputes are concentrated along three sections of her boundary – to the north with the territory of the Afars and Issas (Djibouti), to the west with the Ogaden province of Ethiopia, and to the south-west with the north-eastern province of Kenya, all of which are largely inhabited by Somali. Yet another example of the recent upsurge of boundary problems, as state boundaries begin to act effectively as lines of firm authority, is provided by Uganda, which has attempted to claim back part of western Kenya and part of Sudan. This particular case is remarkable for many reasons, including the fact that it involves raking up the history of boundary-making in this part of Africa over a period of some seventy years; certainly Uganda's facts are right, for when Uganda became independent in 1962 it was only some two-thirds the size it was in 1902. Finally, mention should be made of those boundary problems which represent movements for secession – for instance the attempt of Eritrea to secede from Ethiopia – and involve the setting-up of yet more states on the African continent.

Some of Africa's boundary problems arise from the large number and complex pattern of state territorial units. Even before the recent phase of rapid political change Africa, as politically the most fragmented continent, had the longest land boundaries of any continental group of states: almost 29,000 miles compared with less than 26,000 miles in Asia. As a result, several states are perhaps too small or contain too few people to possess economic, if not political, viability. The kind of economic development a country can follow is obviously related to size and population: a large state like Nigeria has the natural and human resources to strive for a high degree of economic autarchy, should that country so wish, whereas a small country like Gambia will find it difficult, without substantial help from outside, to provide even the basis for an indigenous manufacturing industry. Similarly, a country like Nigeria can safely pursue a much more independent line in politics, either national or international, than can Gambia. Furthermore, many of the states of Africa have five or six immediate neighbours: the Sudan has eight and Zaïre no less than nine. The pattern of nation states also reflects the compactness of the continent and the fact that it has the shortest coastline in relation to area: only Egypt, Morocco, Somalia and South Africa command more than one seaboard. Most of the littoral states have only a narrow coastal front and widen as they extend inland, the most extreme example being Zaïre. Some problems, particularly of transportation, also arise from the awkward shapes of certain states, such as the bow-tie shapes of Mali and Zambia, the L-shape of Somalia, the Katanga pedicle of Zaïre, and the Caprivi Strip of South-West Africa.

The boundaries of many African countries represent colonial extensions from coastal strips or nodes and, as is well illustrated by Nigeria and Gambia, their frontiers reflect the former concentration of trading interests at the coast, the difficulties of inland penetration, and the desire of Europeans to control river mouths. The adoption of watersheds as African boundaries was largely due to the fact that early exploration was often along the rivers, and it was not unusual for colonial powers to agree to adopt a watershed as a boundary before it had even been located or mapped. Where a river or stream was chosen as a boundary, problems have often arisen. In the western Sudan, and especially between Darfur and Wadai, for example, people move to the wadis during the seven to eight months' dry season; yet the boundary between Sudan and Chad was sited for much of its length along the Wadi Kaja and the Wadi Tini. Rather than functioning as a divide, therefore, this section of the boundary acts as a magnet along which and across which there is considerable movement. River boundaries also create difficulties where the waters of the river are harnessed for drinking water, irrigation or hydro-electric power. A good example of this is the Cunene river, with its large and complex schemes, forming the boundary between Angola and South-West Africa; in 1976 South Africa felt obliged to take control of power stations and related works in order to protect the supply of water and power to northern South-West Africa.

Perhaps most publicized are those problems which arise where boundaries pass through the territories of relatively homogeneous ethnic groups. Some of the more striking examples of this phenomenon are provided in Africa, for international boundaries cut through the lands of many large and important ethnic groups – the Hausa, Bakongo, Masai and Somali peoples. In the case of the Azande, these people are dispersed along the Nile–Congo (Zaïre) watershed, 29 per cent of them in Sudan, 68 per cent in Zaïre, and 3 per cent in the Central African Empire.

One of the best-known examples, however, is that of the Ewe, now divided by the southern part of the Ghana–Togo boundary. Today the Ewe problem is believed by some observers to be the main cause of the repeatedly strained relations between Ghana and Togo. Constant friction arises along the international boundary between them, especially where it passes through Eweland. When closed, the frontier interrupts trade, leads to accusations and counter-accusations about the smuggling of arms and subversive elements – though smuggling has always been a feature here at the best of times – and imposes hardship on those communities whose members normally cross the border for seasonal labour or other temporary visits.

The main historical facts about the Ewe problem have been widely discussed and require only the briefest summary here. Living between the Volta and Mono rivers in an area that stretches inland from the coast for over 80 miles in places, the Ewe have been divided between the Germans, British and French in varying ways since the end of the nineteenth century. First, as a result of negotiations between the British and German colonial powers, about four-fifths of Eweland was incorporated into German Togo and one-fifth into the British Gold Coast. Secondly, after the conquest of German Togo by British and French forces in 1914, Eweland was redistributed so that some three-fifths was in British territory and two-fifths in French territory. Thirdly, after the 1914–18 war, yet another adjustment was made, the French area being extended westwards to include the entire coastline of former German Togo. As a result of the mandate agreements of 1919, Eweland was divided into three political elements: two of them under the British (in the Gold Coast and in British-mandated Togo) and one under the French (in the French-mandated area). After the Second World War, the two mandated areas continued to be administered by the British and French respectively as trusteeship territories of the United Nations. Finally, after a plebiscite in 1956, the British trusteeship territory was incorporated into the new independent state of Ghana in 1957, while former French Togo became, in 1960, an independent republic. The Ewe, then, after a most complicated and chequered political history, are today divided between the two independent republics of Ghana and Togo. Since 1960 there have been several disputes over this boundary, and a new conflict has most recently arisen couched, this time, in terms of re-unifying the former German Togo territory – a solution which, if accepted, would simply re-divide another people, the Dagomba. The problem has been further complicated recently by the alleged attempt of a group of Ewe to overthrow the Ghanaian government in an abortive coup.

Internal regional and provincial boundaries can give rise to problems similar to those of national boundaries in Africa. In view of the need to overcome the strong centrifugal forces at work within many African states, the overriding problem of internal boundaries is the extent to which they help or hinder the development of a sense of national unity. In Nigeria a military government, established in 1966, at first abolished all regional boundaries with the aim of dissolving traditional regional allegiances, but in 1967 the country was re-divided by another leader into twelve state units; in 1976 a further division of several of these states gave a new total of nineteen. In Kenya internal divisions resulted in six new, essentially ethnic regions, each of which was originally intended to exercise a measure of administrative autonomy. A seventh, north-eastern region was later added as a concession to the Somali problem; this Kenyan province is occupied largely by Somali nomads who have periodically waged a localized guerrilla war against the Kenyan authorities. But it soon became clear that the projected powers of the seven regions would never be fully exercised, though the divisions still remain. When Zaïre became independent in 1960 it consisted of six large, strongly contrasted provinces, and this number was increased to twenty-two but later reduced to eleven in an attempt to break down regional polarities. In Libya a similar but abortive attempt was made to foster a sense of nationhood by replacing the three large and long-established provinces of Tripolitania, Cyrenaica and Fezzan by ten smaller regions.

To overcome the boundary problems of Africa it has often been suggested that they should be re-drawn 'more in accordance with geographical realities'. But it is difficult to avoid the conclusion that the solution to the problems these 'arbitrary' problems cause must lie not in re-drawing the boundaries, nor in the annexation of one country by another, but in the development of social and economic, if not political, cooperation between neighbouring states. Between Ghana and Togo, for example, the possibilities of some such form of cooperation are obvious: much closer trading links, the joint regulation of tariffs, the reduction of visa and travel requirements, and the improvement of all forms of communication and mobility of labour between the two countries.

There does indeed seem to be an urgent need for much closer practical cooperation between states whose boundaries cut through apparently homogeneous ethnic groups. To achieve this it may be necessary to question two sets of assumptions: first, those held about the nature of the ethnic community in terms of its extent, numbers, composition, coherence and sense of unity; and secondly, those held about the significance of such boundaries. It is perhaps too often assumed that effective national unity is the necessary pre-condition for international cooperation, so that the Ewe problem, for instance, is viewed solely as having a centrifugal effect which works against the growth of national unity and, inevitably, acts as a source of contention between Ghana and Togo.

Yet there are many cases in Africa where the geographically arbitrary nature of a political boundary matters little to the people living on either side of it. Certainly this appears true of the Ewe, most of whom seem content to leave the boundary where it is, and have no strong desire for Ewe unity as such. The Ghanaian Ewe think of themselves first as Ghanaian and secondly as Ewe: the Togolese Ewe think of themselves first as Togolese. What these people object to is not that they live in one country rather than another but that they are cut off from their farms, their kinsmen and their sources of seasonal labour every time the boundary is closed by one of the two governments. The need here, as in most parts of Africa, is to concentrate attention not on the academic analysis of former colonial boundaries or present state boundaries, nor on how to re-draw the political boundaries more in accordance with 'geographical realities', but on ways of ensuring that boundaries function solely as the territorial limits of administrations and not as barriers to movement and contact between states. While the realities of the Ewe and similar problems in Africa support the argument for leaving the national state boundaries as they are, they do at the same time indicate some of the opportunities for creating larger regional groupings for the purposes of social and economic development: in Nyerere's words, 'we must use the existing pattern of states as an instrument for unifying Africa and not as an instrument for dividing Africa'. [8]

However unsatisfactory on academic or indeed practical grounds the existing pattern of states in Africa may be, there is general acceptance of the old colonial boundaries as frameworks for the nation states of today. Where so-called 'boundary problems' in Africa are said to exist, they commonly reveal a deep-rooted conflict between states and are used to express a friction generated by some other cause or for some other purpose. The decision by the Organization for African Unity that no attempt should be made to change the existing state boundaries is clearly realistic. First, there is the historical fact that colonial governments were only prepared to hand over

35

power on a territorial basis and at different times; this formalized and perpetuated the old colonial divisions. Moreover, the political élites in all African countries naturally enough set out to establish their influence within existing territorial areas; their approach was inevitably pragmatic and they subsequently found it easier to work within the framework inherited from the colonial powers. Secondly, it is generally appreciated that no alternative political map would be generally more acceptable than the present map: the complex and fluid pattern of the indigenous, pre-colonial social and political systems could never provide an adequate territorial basis for independence in the modern world. Finally, no changing of a boundary can take place without infringing the existing and so recently won sovereignty of one or more other states.

Yet it is important to recognize that this point of view is by no means so universally accepted as the pronouncements of OAU and many African government leaders might suggest. Several African states are beginning to argue that there is no reason why national boundaries in Africa should be thought of as immutable. Uganda, Togo and Somalia, for instance, have all recently challenged the 'sacrosanct principle of the immutability of African frontiers' where it does not stand up to what is termed 'objective historical analysis'. Moreover there are cases in recent years of small boundary changes taking place without conflict. Senegal has agreed to re-draw slightly the boundary between Senegal and Gambia, handing over to Gambia an area including twenty-six villages in the Kantona region.

As a general rule, however, there is everything to be said for maintaining the existing pattern of nation states of Africa. The fact that existing boundaries cut across 'geographical regions' or areas 'with similar physical, social or economic conditions' need not necessarily be interpreted as an obstacle to national unity. Whether this is true of those countries whose boundaries appear to leave them peculiarly disadvantaged – the landlocked states of Africa – is another matter.

36

The landlocked states

The importance of the landlocked state issue in Africa reflects the facts that fourteen out of the world's twenty-eight landlocked states are in Africa, and that they occupy about a quarter of the continent's area and contain almost 15 per cent of its population. With their colonial experience, most African states still have a great trade dependency on the western world: trade is still oriented externally rather than internally, only 7 per cent of Africa's imports coming from, and only 6 per cent of Africa's exports going to, other African countries. With this stark fact the landlocked states are peculiarly ill-equipped to deal, and its legal, psychological and political, let alone economic implications have been widely debated.

Before looking at their specific problems, however, it is important to establish the very varied nature of African landlocked states. There are a few countries which are nearly landlocked, the most important and obvious being Zaïre; and, as we shall discover in a later chapter, Zaïre *feels* itself to be landlocked today as much as any completely landlocked country. But of the fourteen fully landlocked states in Africa, depending wholly on neighbouring transit states for access to the sea, seven are Francophone and seven Anglophone (see the map on p. ii). Of the seven Francophone states, five are contiguous and curve round in an arc eastwards from Mali, Upper Volta and Niger to Chad and thence southwards to the Central African Empire. These five states, formerly part of French West Africa or French Equatorial Africa, were of course never intended to operate as separate economic units; the French colonial policy, it will be recalled, was designed to coordinate their various contiguous territories within a single economic system. The other two Francophone landlocked states are Rwanda and Burundi, which lie on the western edge of the East African plateau and were formerly administered by Belgium under the trusteeship arrangement with the United Nations. Rwanda is exceptional in that it is in a sense 'doubly landlocked', all its outlets being through Uganda, itself landlocked. The seven Anglophone states include Uganda in the north and, further south, the four contiguous states of Zambia, Malawi, Rhodesia and Botswana. Finally there are the two tiny states of Swaziland and, completely embedded in South Africa, Lesotho. Lesotho, indeed, provides perhaps the extreme case of a landlocked state. That the present picture of landlocked states in Africa is by no means static, however, is clear from the case of Ethiopia. Ethiopia was landlocked until 1952 when the addition of Eritrea gave the country an outlet, albeit only to the Red Sea, and the effect of any successful secession of Eritrea from Ethiopia would of course be to make Ethiopia once again a landlocked nation.

In discussing landlocked states in Africa there is also the complication of the existence of internal states in, for instance, Nigeria, where fifteen out of the nineteen states of the Federal Republic are landlocked. The problems of such 'internal' landlocked states are in some respects similar to those of national landlocked states, but in the case of the former the problems are different in intensity in that they are ameliorated by the existence of common currencies, tariffs and an allegiance to a common national identity. Then parts of some states are almost landlocked: the Casamance region of southern Senegal and the Caprivi Strip of South-West Africa are cases in point. And even coastal states may depend on ports other than their own; until the recent closure of her border with Sierra Leone, for instance, Guinea exported her cattle and imported many of her consumer goods through Sierra Leone's port of Freetown, which serves a large part of Guinea more conveniently than can her own port of Conakry. In other cases, transit trade is necessary because of inadequate facilities for specialized goods; until the modern port of Cotonou was opened in 1964, for example, Dahomey (Benin) could not handle large imports of oil, which had to be imported through Lagos and brought along the coastal lagoon system of waterways. In the Sudan, congestion at Port Sudan and an overloaded road and rail system make it necessary for the southern region of the Sudan to import goods through Mombasa and Uganda.

One other complication tends to obscure clear discussion of the landlocked state issue in Africa. This is that there are very different degrees of landlockedness – compare, for instance, Swaziland and Rwanda. This is an important point, for it can be argued that landlockedness, like a boundary, only becomes a problem where conflict between states has already been engendered by some other cause. As Hermans has put it for Botswana,

> the hypothesis which Botswana seems to verify is that the problems confronting landlocked states, like those of island states, stem not so much from the fact of their geographical situation as from the character of the environment which surrounds them – whether it is hostile or friendly, whether it encourages isolation or contact, whether it creates opportunities for internal development or drains domestic resources.[9]

The changing nature of landlockedness is indeed well shown in southern Africa as a whole. This southern geopolitical zone is still almost as interdependent as it was in the past. Zambia now has rail, road and oil-pipeline access to the east coast at Dar es Salaam. But both Zaïre and Zambia have temporarily lost their more important access to the west coast by the Benguela railway. As a result Zaïre, especially Katanga, is more landlocked than ever. Zambia is considerably worse off, for the Portuguese had increased the capacity of the Benguela railway. Rhodesia has lost its important coastal outlets to Beira and Maputo, as well as the Botswana section of its line to the south; but it has added the Beit Bridge rail link to South Africa and now depends entirely on that.

The problems of landlocked states in Africa, as elsewhere, arise basically from the need for free and secure access to the high seas. The legal position on this point is highly complex and by no means generally agreed. There is a clear division of opinion between those who believe that right of free access to the sea for all is supportable in international law, and those who believe that such right must be achieved by negotiation. At the practical level this division is largely between the landlocked countries, which claim access to the sea as a right in international law, and many coastal states which insist that this right is of a contractual and therefore revocable nature. A great deal has been written on the practical problems such a conflict of opinion raises. Zambia's difficulties in exporting her copper received great publicity and led to the building of the Tan-Zam railway by the Chinese; now that Mozambique is independent, links through that country are being proposed, including a rail link from Luanda, through Feira to enter Mozambique at Zumbo, and a road link from Katete in Zambia to Bene in Mozambique. In Chad there are four main outlets ranging in length from 1,100 to 2,000 miles. Nine of the fourteen landlocked states have direct rail links with an ocean port (Botswana, Lesotho, Malawi, Mali, Rhodesia, Swaziland, Uganda, Upper Volta and Zambia); three others have to use road transport to reach a rail head (Chad, Niger and Rwanda); two countries use river and lake transport to reach a rail head (Burundi and the Central African Empire); and one state (Zambia) now has direct road links with an ocean port.

This problem of links through transit states to coastal ports is partly an economic matter, and the economic costs of being landlocked are many and obvious. But there are also severe political costs for landlocked countries in their dependence on other states. And yet this relationship is by no means simple or one-sided. The relationship between a large and economically powerful landlocked country, like Rhodesia, and a relatively smaller and weaker country on the coast is very different from that which exists between a landlocked state and its equally or more powerful transit state. In analysing the consequences for a landlocked country it is crucial to bear in mind the relativity of power between it and its principal transit state. Moreover, this relativity is continually changing. In the case of Rhodesia, for instance, contemporary events are rapidly increasing the degree of landlockedness. The northern rail link through Zambia has long been closed and, as a result of the independence of Mozambique, the two eastern rail links to Beira and Maputo are currently denied to Rhodesia; this, of course, represents part of the attempt to force Rhodesia into accepting black majority rule and to hasten the end of that country's unilateral declaration of independence. The new Mozambique government has been promised compensation by Britain and other countries for the loss of revenue to Mozambique such action causes. Now that Botswana has also decided to withhold permission to use the Botswana rail link, Rhodesia has become dependent on only one rail link via the Beit Bridge route to South African ports.

The various problems of African landlocked states may be tackled in several ways. One is to create *ad hoc* bilateral agreements between a landlocked state and its transit coastal neighbour. Examples of these agreements are many and varied and include, for instance, the convention between Mali and Ivory Coast concerning the establishment of rebates on long-distance transport to and from Mali by the Abidjan–Niger Railway Administration; another example is the Order in Council of Niger concerning the Common Rail and Road Transport Services of Niger and Dahomey. Such conventions, orders in council or agreements are directed primarily at securing the use of land transport facilities. But of equal and, perhaps, of potentially greater importance is air transport. While international air arrangements require that overflying rights be obtained before the air space of another country may be entered, such a form of transport is, according to many authorities, of particular value to landlocked states in Africa. Distances are great, population densities are generally very low, the costs of good rail and road works and their maintenance are commonly beyond the resources of landlocked countries, whilst air transport has the great advantage of requiring very much lower capital outlays in this respect. Especially if the goods to be carried are of high value, then air transport is in many ways to be preferred. Air transport in Africa is not necessarily a luxury. Mali is a good example of a country which has made effective use of air transport, 75 per cent of her meat exports leaving the country by air. Air transport has its political implications, too; Lesotho has asked China for aid to build an international airport near Maseru to avoid the need to depend on Johannesburg in the Republic of South Africa. Such a development of air transport must have profound effects on the economic and psychological isolation of land-locked states.

A second means of reducing the ill-effects of landlockedness is to reduce a country's dependence on external trade – in other words to restructure the internal economy of a landlocked state so that it faces its geographical realities, strives to become more self-sufficient, and so is less dependent on its transit state. But a third solution is, in the opinion of most writers, the most practical. This is to overcome the problem of landlockedness by establishing reciprocal economic institutions, sometimes backed by multinational treaties. Many of the landlocked states in Africa belong to or have belonged to some form of grouping for economic cooperation, such as the East African Community, Union Douanière et Économique de l'Afrique Centrale (UDEAC) and the Economic Community of West African States (ECOWAS). More will be said of such regional groupings in a later chapter, but it is worth noting here that the OAU has been asked to direct its activities at sponsoring such groupings on the basis of every state having the right of free access to the sea.

Bilateral agreements, together with a greater development of air transport; a restructuring of the internal economies so that they depend less on external trade and more on internal production and consumption; and cooperation between states in regional economic unions of one form or another – these are widely believed to be the three possible means of salvation for the fourteen landlocked countries of Africa. And yet experience suggests that, given the fierce nationalism of most states, these are unrealistic or at best only long-term solutions. Perhaps the only immediately effective solution is for each landlocked state to face the stark realities of its own particular geography and location and act accordingly. The dilemma which such a view presents may be illustrated from southern Africa where the whole landlocked issue is inexorably bound up with the ques-tion of race. As one writer has put it, to be landlocked is difficult enough; to be black and landlocked in southern Africa is a lonely and expensive experience. In Malawi, Banda has in the past followed a severely realistic and pragmatic policy towards Rhodesia and South Africa. To some extent the same was true of Botswana until very recently. Seretse Khama's views on this are significant: '. . . we decided never to ignore the harsh realities of our situation as an integral part of South Africa. We cannot pick up our vast country and replace it on some more comfortable portion of the map.'[10] This, perhaps, sums it all up.

3 Ethnicity and élitism
in Africa

Ethnicity

We have already had occasion to refer to the ethnic group –
or 'tribe' as it used to be called before that term acquired
derogatory connotations in Africa – as an important factor in
the analysis of African affairs. And some observers would point
to this factor as the most common root cause of Africa's
problems today. But how does one define the ethnic group?
All definitions include the notion of a group with some kind
of corporate identity or allegiance. The ethnic group connotes
loyalty to a group which is politically independent; it also
expresses loyalty to a common culture which parallels or trans-
cends loyalty to the state.

As a social structure capable of fulfilling the basic life needs
of its members, the *ethnic group* is considered by some authorities to be disappearing as an important factor in Africa,
especially in urban and 'modernized' areas. But *ethnicity*, in
the sense of identification, psychological commitment, historical

membership, or set of shared values, is considered to remain important everywhere. However one defines it, ethnicity is clearly not a peculiarly African phenomenon, being found in both developing and developed countries, past and present; in the United Kingdom, for instance, the Welsh are as clearly a 'tribe' or 'ethnic' group as are the Kikuyu of Kenya. Moreover, ethnicity takes a variety of forms and expresses itself in different intensities. While some groups, like the Yoruba of south-western Nigeria, have a strongly centralized political system, others, like the Ibo of south-eastern Nigeria, have a highly segmented and diffuse village-based political system; others, again, are virtually without rulers of any kind. One widely accepted classification of ethnic groups distinguishes between two types of societies. One consists of those societies which have centralized authority, administrative machinery and judicial institutions – in short, a government – and in which cleavages of wealth, rank or privileged status correspond to the distribution of power and authority; examples of such societies are the Banyakole, Bembe, Ngwato, Yoruba and Zulu. The other type lacks centralized authority, administrative machinery and judicial institutions – in short, it *lacks* government – and possesses no sharp divisions of rank, status or wealth; examples are the Logoli, Nuer and Tallensi.

There are also important differences between sedentary groups and those nomadic groups which travel widely over vast geographical areas. And a group's size may vary enormously, ranging from a few families travelling together to groups with populations of over 10,000,000 – ethnic groups which would seem almost to approximate to nations in themselves. Again, it is difficult to compare usefully the ethnicity of peoples in the copperbelt of Zambia, where the whole issue is bound up with urbanization, élitism and race, with the kind of ethnicity referred to earlier in our comments on the Ewe in West Africa. There is, as Cohen has put it, ethnicity and ethnicity:

the constraints that custom exercises on the individual vary from case to case. Because of its ubiquity, variety of form, scope and intensity, and of its involvement in psychic, social and historical variables, ethnicity has been defined in a variety of ways, depending on the discipline, field experience and interests of the investigator.[11]

Such general remarks require some illustration. Different maps of the ethnic groups or societies of Africa often reveal quite startling differences, and it is only at the level of almost meaningless generalization that they have any validity. The problem is partly one of scale. Take the case of Morocco. According to most general maps of Africa there are some fifteen ethnic groups in Morocco, but according to Mikesell's more specialized map of that country there are several hundred groups in the same area. Clearly the compilers of these maps are thinking at quite different scales and are applying very different criteria for establishing their ethnic units. At the level of the town or village an even more complex and detailed pattern of ethnic distributions may be made. The assumptions that the territorial area covered by an ethnic group is culturally homogeneous and that a boundary line can be drawn around an ethnic area on the ground are both demonstrably false.

In the case of the Yoruba of south-western Nigeria and southern Benin, for instance, the term Yorubaland is commonly thought of as a cultural region, though as usually defined it refers more to a language group than to a true cultural or racial group. The different sub-groups of the Yoruba are clearly identified, geographically, culturally and politically. Moreover, only in the centre of Yorubaland does the population average more than 70 per cent Yoruba, and this is known as the 'core region' of Yorubaland, where Yoruba culture is most typically to be found. Nevertheless there is, in the field at least, a clear consensus of opinion about where Yoruba country ends and where, for instance, the Fon, Nupe, Igbirra and Edo areas begin. But three reservations need to be made here. First, there are places where the density of population is so low as to make any decision difficult to reach, and this is especially true of the Yoruba in the northern and north-western limits, where some authorities would extend the boundary to include the

Sabe group of the Yoruba in north-central Benin. Secondly, there is a certain amount of overlapping of peoples around the edges of Yoruba country, especially in the north where the Yoruba are geographically mixed with the Fulani and Nupe. Thirdly, there is a large number of important non-Yoruba groups within Yorubaland, forming especially important elements in the main towns and coastal regions. It is clear, then, that the idea of a homogeneous ethnic group occupying a distinct and discrete geographical area has little validity in the case of the Yoruba, and the same is broadly true of most other so-called ethnic group areas in Africa.

We have already noted the relevance of Africa's historical experience to ethnicity. Some groups, like the Ewe, are split by international boundaries. Another example of this very common phenomenon is afforded by the Bakongo who, living astride the mouth of the Congo (Zaïre) river, were divided between Portuguese Angola, the Belgian Congo and the French Congo. In other cases groups, even those which have been traditionally fiercely antagonistic towards each other, have been lumped together within the same colonial territory. Thus in Nigeria the Muslim Hausa/Fulani of the north were placed within the same state as their traditional enemies of central Nigeria, as well as with the Yoruba, Ibo and other groups of the south.

This is a most important point for, according to some writers, an element of interaction is believed to be essential to ethnicity and the degree of ethnicity depends therefore on the degree of interaction between one ethnic group and another. Ethnicity, unlike an ethnic group, cannot exist in isolation. It is sometimes suggested, indeed, that ethnicity, as distinct from the notion of an ethnic group, is essentially the product of the colonial period, when conflict and interaction was forced upon African peoples. For example, the Fon of Benin, according to Argyle, 'had to be taught that they belonged' to an ethnic group;[12] and further east in Nigeria the Church Missionary Society missionaries developed their Yoruba mission, applying the term 'Yoruba' to an area vastly larger than that occupied by the Yoruba proper and, through education in the mission schools and by writing down and formalizing the language, helped to create or at least foster the sense of being a Yoruba. Again, the Ibo concept of themselves as a distinctive group is very much a twentieth-century phenomenon, the result of external pressures and European contacts. In many cases there may be some truth in the contention that the European colonial period created or encouraged ethnicity. But one must not ignore the fact that ethnicity, resulting from interaction or conflict, certainly existed in pre-colonial days. And in independent Africa today there is no evidence of a decrease in ethnicity – rather the reverse. In Uganda, for instance, it has been observed that the Gisu only became conscious of themselves as an ethnic group with a corporate identity or common loyalty when they began to feel threatened by the numerous and powerful Baganda.

A further characteristic of ethnicity is that it is not, and never can be, a purely static phenomenon: the multi-cellular pattern of African social groups is very much alive, each cell expanding or contracting, strengthening or weakening as the case may be. It is possible, of course, for the essential conflict to work either for or against ethnicity. One writer has shown how in some cases class cleavages work with or are coincident with ethnic divisions, as with the Creoles of Sierra Leone, the Tutsi of Burundi or the Americo-Liberians of Liberia; in such cases ethnicity is hardened and confirmed. But where, as is perhaps much more common in Africa, class cleavages cut right across ethnic divisions, then the conflicts may develop more along class than along ethnic lines. Class, in these situations, may eventually become more powerful and significant than the ethnic group, and the lower classes of two contiguous ethnic groups may well unite in opposition to the combined strengths of their two upper-class groups. This is believed to be especially true in conditions of urbanization, where the processes of change are more rapid and relatively easy to observe.

The case of the city of Ibadan in Nigeria is therefore worth looking at, for it enables us to reduce the scale of analysis to that of the urban centre. Here in Ibadan – an indigenous

Yoruba town of about 1,000,000 inhabitants – the Muslim Hausa and Western Ibo are two important non-indigenous groups and in the early 1920s both were allocated specific residential districts. Since that time both groups have been subjected to the same forces, pressures and opportunities. But today, as Cohen as shown,[13] the two groups present marked contrasts. The Hausa have preserved, indeed deepened, their cultural distinctiveness; for the most part they still speak only Hausa and interact socially only among themselves. A cleavage, sometimes a tense cleavage, exists between them and the host communities in Ibadan. The Western Ibo, on the other hand, have almost lost their cultural distinctiveness over the same period. Their residential segregation has completely broken down and their compounds are occupied by peoples from different ethnic groups. They did have a group association – the Western Ibo Union of Ibadan – but it was a weak association; it met only once a month; and it suffered from embezzlement of funds and from frequent quarrels amongst its members. Moreover, like many other tribal associations in Africa, the Western Ibo Union did not aim at any exclusive ethnic policy but was concerned solely to promote the successful adaptation of its members to modern urban conditions. Whereas everything within the Hausa group was aimed at maintaining the distinctiveness of the Hausa, among the Western Ibo exactly the opposite occurred. The Western Ibo are now indistinguishable from the largely Yoruba majority. The second-generation Western Ibo speak Yoruba and often cannot speak Ibo at all and they, unlike the Hausa, frequently intermarry with the Yoruba and other groups.

This example of Cohen's identifies the two extremes of a continuum – at the one end an ethnic group (in this case the Western Ibo) which loses its cultural distinctiveness and indeed wishes to do so; and at the other end the Hausa, who are determined to retain their distinctiveness and cultural autonomy. In the one case an ethnic group reacts to outside pressures by adjustment, assimilation and adaptation; in the other case the ethnic group reorganizes and redefines its own traditional customs or develops new customs under traditional symbols.

49

Why there should be this difference in reaction is an interesting question which we cannot pursue here. Some writers would explain it in terms of inherent differences in character and temperament between the thrusting, ambitious Ibo and the conservative, traditional Hausa. But such an explanation is certainly far too simplistic.

In trying to evaluate ethnicity in the contemporary African scene, it will be apparent that it can have both negative and positive effects. As for the negative effects, the examples of these are numerous and generally obvious. In Zaïre a major problem is believed to be the large number of groups (over 200) and the dominance of four of them – the Bakongo, Balunda, Bamongo and Baluba. And in Nigeria the mutual antagonisms of the Muslim Hausa and Fulani in the north and the Yoruba and Ibo in the south have made any sense of Nigerian national unity peculiarly difficult to achieve. In many cases party politics are based on the ethnic group, so that in some states any change in government is taken as an ethnic alternative.

In the Congo, until a Marxist government took over, the ethnic basis of politics was clearly evident. The Bakongo group is dominant in this country of only about 1,500,000 people and they spread out over the international boundaries into Zaïre and Angola. Within Congo Brazzaville each of the three main political parties formerly represented one of the three major ethnic groups – Bakongo, M'Bochi and Vili – and each of these was supported by one or more of the many religious sects which flourish in the area. In some states, as with the Kikuyu of Kenya, the political role of the dominant group is believed to make national cohesion difficult to achieve. Again, this is a clearly dynamic feature. In Uganda, for instance, the previous political dominance of the Baganda in the south was removed by the Amin government which filled all senior government and military posts with Nilotic northerners – either Kakwa people like himself or other small groups on whose loyalty he could depend; ethnicity was also used to retain power by oppression of two other northern groups – the Acholi and the Langa, the group to which Obote, the former president now in Tanzania, belongs. Moreover, secession movements within states (Biafra in Nigeria), territorial expansion (the Somali in Somalia) and the emergence of one-party states (Zambia): all have been explained, however superficially and misleadingly, in terms of ethnicity. In Algeria, too, the ancient cleavage between Arab and Berber finds expression in the internal politics of the country. And in Sudan, whilst most of the northern peoples are Arabicized and have come under the unifying influence of Islam, the diverse peoples of the south have remained ethnically distinct and politically fragmented. Even large groups, like the Dinka, lack a unified system of government. It is also easy to point to the effects ethnicity has in encouraging nepotism – in government, commerce, business and education – and in curbing the initiative and motivation of the individual through the persistence of such social institutions as the extended family system.

On the other hand, ethnicity is a fact and is deeply embedded in African life, culture, society and economy; it cannot just be removed or suppressed. Moreover, many writers emphasize the positive effects of ethnicity. It can be argued that ethnicity is often blamed for difficulties that are much more deeply rooted. Perhaps ethnicity, like a boundary or landlockedness, is rarely the root cause of instability but is used or manipulated by politicians for their own purposes. Indeed, the balancing of one ethnic group against another has been shown to be a force for good. This kind of ethnic arithmetic may be essential for good government: Houphöuet-Boigny in Ivory Coast, Senghor in Senegal, Nyerere in Tanzania, Kaunda in Zambia and Kenyatta in Kenya – all have so far been able to balance out the ambitions and fears of different ethnic groups by making carefully chosen appointments. Nyerere, in particular, has quite explicitly utilized the qualities of each group in the positive task of nation-building. In this sense ethnicity can play a largely constructive role in the creation of national unity. For, after all, is ethnicity not just one form of allegiance? Some form of allegiance or focus of loyalty seems to be essential in creating any effective nation state. Ethnicity can also be an asset in modernization in that it enlarges the sense of collective identity and security at different levels and can maintain links between town and country. A member of a particular ethnic group coming to a town will, initially at least, develop his links with the social network of his own home area. Complete and rapid destruction of ethnic identity is the exception rather than the rule in Africa.

In evaluating ethnicity a rather different approach is to argue from the distinction made earlier between the ethnic group and ethnicity, and to conclude that the group, as a focus for corporate identity and common loyalty, may well be a positive force for good; but that ethnicity, or the force which derives from conflict and tends to be defensive and parochial, is undesirable and nothing less than a particularly virulent form of nationalism.

In any evaluation of ethnicity, however, the dangers of oversimplification are very great; it is usually a very complex issue, as the case of Burundi eloquently illustrates. Burundi is one of the states originally established by the Germans but later mandated by the League of Nations to Belgium, which later administered the territory under the United Nations Trusteeship Council. Lying on the north-eastern shore of Lake Tanganyika, it is a densely populated country with some 3,700,000 inhabitants. It is landlocked, depending entirely on Tanzania for its outlets. Within Burundi there are two major ethnic groups – the Tutsi (about 16 per cent of the total population) and the Hutu (the remaining 84 per cent). The Tutsi may be further sub-divided into two groups, the higher-caste Tutsi Banyaraguru group in the north, and the lower-caste Tutsi Hima in the south. The latter – Tutsi Hima – are, however, the dominant group politically – the political élite as distinct from the traditional high-caste élite of the Tutsi Banyaraguru. In an attempt to break the powerful political position of the Tutsi Hima, the Tutsi Banyaraguru are believed to have made an alliance with the Hutu majority. The attempt failed, and reprisals were exacted by the Tutsi Hima against the Hutu in May and June 1972. The Tutsi Hima concentrated on savage reprisals against the Hutu élite – in schools, the university, in administration and in business – massacring about 3·5 per cent of the total population. As the Minority

Rights Group report of 1974 states: '. . . this is the outstanding example of selective genocide' in which the actual and potential intellectual élite among the Hutu was destroyed. Burundi therefore became perhaps the only country in Africa to claim the appurtenances of a genuine class society, a country in which power is the monopoly of a dominant ethnic minority and where the Hutu are clearly second-class citizens. The Hutu were then legally excluded from the army, civil service, and any kind of university or secondary education. How exactly the military coup in Burundi in November 1976 changed this situation is unclear.

The case of Burundi is illuminating because it conflicts markedly with the situation in Rwanda where the same ethnic divisions occur but where no such oppression has taken place. Clearly it is not simply the existence of two ethnic groups within a country that has caused the conflict. And it may be that the element of interaction or conflict between them is determined more by the élite sections of the groups than by the mass of the group populations. This notion fits in with a definition of ethnicity as 'the competitive struggle for modernization between the élite members of different ethnic groups'. The case of Burundi certainly underlines the difficulty of disentangling ethnicity from the wider and more complex issues of structural cleavages, notably élitism. And it is to this question of élitism that we must now turn.

Élitism

An élite may be defined as a group which influences power and clearly re-defines the norms of society. Other definitions include that of an élite as 'a group which gets the best of what's going'. An élite is also defined as a group which enjoys a position of pre-eminence over others which is shown by various acts of deference; the élite should also have some degree of corporateness and exclusiveness, with definite barriers to admission. Whichever definition one accepts, the élite clearly forms a very different kind of group from the ethnic group, though there are circumstances in which ethnic

53

élitism occurs – when, for instance, there is some coincidence between an ethnic group, sub-group or clan and its role as an élite group.

Historically there has long existed the pre-colonial or 'traditional élite'. Such élites in Africa were usually chiefs or priests, influential men or wealthy traders who either influenced activity or exerted power in one way or another. These traditional élite groups were, and commonly still are, relatively conservative and often illiterate, though this varies very much from case to case. To attempt to compare strongly centralized and hierarchical groups like the Hausa with the élitist and nomadic Tuareg, with a very decentralized group like the Ibo, or with those societies without chiefs or rulers of any kind, shows how difficult it is to compare them usefully in structural terms. The concept of the traditional élite, then, does not necessarily involve a strongly centralized authority – the power of a chief. In some cases, too, the traditional political élite is external in origin as with the Azande, upon whom the Avung-dra imposed their political control, membership of the élite being prescribed by birth. And among the Nuer the traditional élite group is perhaps better described as the dominant lineage, from among whose members ritual leaders are selected.

The 'colonial élite' is still seen today in those parts of Africa where there are substantial numbers of Europeans and in those parts of Africa where the European set up an African élite group or society, as with the Creoles of Sierra Leone. But here again generalization is not easy. One has to compare élitism in those countries, such as South Africa or Rhodesia, where Europeans settled to become South Africans or Rhodesians, with élitism in, for instance, British West Africa, where the British did not go to settle permanently and where, moreover, the desire to become a Gambian or Nigerian never played an important part in Europeans' attitudes. Then in the former Belgian Congo, now Zaïre, there was virtually no encouragement of an indigenous élite. As already pointed out, Belgian colonial policy eschewed any attempt to create an African middle class, though this was envisaged in the long term. Whereas the former Belgian Congo at independence in 1960 had only

7 graduates and Tanzania about 100, Nigeria had some 10,000. It is also important to point out that colonial élites among Africans were often quite consciously created by colonial administrators in their preference for certain ethnic groups to fulfil certain roles – for instance in the army – so intensifying and concentrating early modernization.

During the post-colonial period there is no doubt that the 'new élite' has in many cases tended to become more or less identical to the élites effected during the European colonial period. This involves Africans adopting the former European colonial ways of life – their manners, ways of speaking, dress, attitudes and languages. Indeed, some observers would claim that one of the characteristic features of such African élites today is that many of them are more like Europeans than the European ever was. It is also highly important to appreciate the speed of change here, many of the educated élite in Africa today having been born to poor, illiterate peasants. A related issue is how far class and the 'new élites' are the same. Many writers have argued that class simply represents a new form of élitism in Africa; this follows as a result of the 'detribalization' of Africans, especially as they move into the towns. But according to Cohen, classes are 'the figments of the imagination of sociologists'.[14] He argues that what actually exist in Africa are large numbers of interest groups, at different scales and at different levels of political significance, which can be ranged on a continuum from the most formally organized to the least formally organized with, predictably, most groups lying somewhere in-between. What is important here is the degree of formal organization which may be expressed in the concentration of one interest group in a particular part of a town or country, rather than the question of class. Cohen argues further that the notion of class in the Marxist sense does not really exist in most African countries, in spite of their colonial experience.

So far a distinction has been drawn between the 'traditional', 'colonial' and 'new' élites of Africa. But, like all classifications, it does not cover every case. Élites in Africa can also be categorized according to the degree of emulation they inspire in those who do not belong; they can often be distinguished in this way because the gap in the alien cultures or sections within a society is so wide that all modes of behaviour within one separate group appear similar to the outsider. One or two of the most distinctive features go to make up the stereotype of particular élites. The uppermost category is what has been called the standard setting group. Commonly, however, the term élite, when applied to a particular country, refers to a single group, sometimes an actual ethnic group, simply because the standards of living in the area where they live and their educational experiences are similar and appear to be superior. It is possible to distinguish many such categories but, with the rapidity of social change and the different opportunities for acquiring élite status, the categories undoubtedly become both less distinct and more numerous. Nevertheless, the stratification of African society in this manner is obviously a direct result of European occupation, the ensuing rapid industrialization and urbanization and the resulting conflicts with the traditional rulers or chiefs.

Lloyd distinguishes three important categories of élites.[15] First there is the traditional élite, generally conservative and illiterate. Then there is the upper-middle class or intelligentsia, which is wealthy, literate, 'detribalized' and westernized. Thirdly there is the lower middle-class or 'sub-intelligentsia', which is most closely identified with the mass of the population and their aspirations. Today in Africa this third group has often given rise to sub-groups – the political élite or the military élite. Sometimes, however, the political or military élite may arise quite independently, more particularly as education no longer becomes the sole qualification for acquiring élite status. Using Lloyd's classification, therefore, there are three major competing élite groups representing respectively the traditional values, westernized values and an attempted marriage of the two. The new political élites in Africa are probably the most powerful and the most emulated. The traditional élite is by far the least powerful. The intelligentsia hold the most important jobs in law, the civil service and medicine – jobs which are now competed for to a much greater extent as a higher percentage of the population passes through secondary and higher education, whereas during the colonial period in most African countries this kind of occupation was the preserve of the European.

Generally there is great confusion from within and without of the various rankings of the élites, so that one cannot really rank them in a hierarchical sense from the professional élite or the intelligentsia at the top down to the mass or 'sub-intelligentsia' at the base. And this confusion has led some people to distinguish even more categories of élites. One author distinguishes five élite groups, the main change here being a distinction between the middle class and what are called the revolutionary intellectuals; in other words, the author objects to the idea that the intelligentsia really comprises a homogeneous group. Another writer finds it necessary to distinguish what he calls the 'wealthy illiterate trader'. This again is a breakdown, in this case of the traditional élite; but it is admitted that this sub-group, largely composed of women, is undergoing rapid change and within a few years will hardly be distinguishable as a separate corporate group, at least in southern Nigeria among the Yoruba women long-distance traders, who constitute a very powerful group in financial, economic and political terms.

Turning now to the role élites play in Africa, their major role is believed by many writers to be in stimulating the growth of the economy and has been likened to the role played by entrepreneurs in the industrialization of north-western Europe in the nineteenth century. The élite groups are in touch with European or international trading networks and, as a result of the prestige they command over the mass of the population, they help to diffuse new ideas and modes of living throughout a country. Through the intermediaries of the élites new ideas may seem attractive and worth emulating, and without this in-between group with its distinctive role, the diffusion of ideas would probably be much slower and less widespread. In other words, the existence of an élite has made economic development more possible, social integration easier and modernization more feasible. Élites, in this sense, have an important 'civilizing' effect. South Africa is an instance where the original European élite acquired prestige because of its immense superiority in the technological and economic fields.

Élites may also act as innovators, the Creoles of Sierra Leone being an example. Today the innovating role of the Creoles has passed but their power is still significant, and occupationally they have had a very élitist role to play in the capital of Freetown. They were an important élite group in the nineteenth century. Originally they were freed slaves and so had very few skills, but, located on the Sierra Leone peninsula and in Freetown, they were able to seize new opportunities for commerce and subsequent political office. Many of these Creoles prospered in trade or as clerks in government offices and, with the aid of education, especially from the missionaries, formed themselves into a closed and powerful élite. Later the ascendancy of the Creoles in trade declined as expatriate companies, especially British companies, took over; but because the Creoles had invested their money in property and because of the form of education they gave to their children, closely following the European way of life and European values, they were able to maintain their prestigious position. The Creoles have influenced the architecture, urban administration, and the location of different racial and class groups in the city. They used to live in the wealthy houses in central Freetown but subsequently moved out to the suburbs and are not now found as discrete elements, being mixed with the suburban group generally. The indigenous population in and around Freetown soon saw that the road to prosperity and power lay in their attaining education in order to qualify for the professions and power attained by the Creoles. The Creoles were, until recently, known as 'Black Englishmen' and they have mostly adopted or acquired English names. The role of the Creoles in the economic and social development of Sierra Leone, then, is an indirect but vital one. By their mode of living, by the standards they set themselves, by the kinds of houses they live in, they set new standards and ambitions for the mass of the population to emulate.

Linked to this is the specific role élites play in fostering trade, both within their own countries and with outside partners. The very fact that élite groups have standards to maintain means new demands for an increasing variety of products. In Nigeria, where independence was a relatively lengthy process, the trading patterns established by the colonial administrators were maintained after independence in 1960 and were even expanded by the new élites of Nigeria. Likewise the élites have often been responsible for introducing new crops and new farming techniques.

The role of the political élite, particularly the nationalist leaders, has also been vital. But problems have sometimes arisen where the political élite has been responsible for the initiation of development planning and for the precise location of industries, agricultural schemes and new plantations. Usually completely out of touch with the intelligentsia or traditional élite, the political élite may make fundamental decisions about planning irrigation schemes, often without scientific or educated understanding of the problems involved. This is perhaps especially true of Uganda, whose military élite is largely uneducated whereas Uganda has an exceptionally large pool of well-educated Africans who are unable to affect materially the decisions made by the government.

The implications of élitism can perhaps best be illustrated by looking at the phenomenon at a range of scales from the national scale right down to the level of the local village or village group. Economically by far the most élitist state in Africa is South Africa. Among black African governments perhaps the most successful states economically are Ivory Coast and Nigeria. Then there are those states, of which Tanzania is the most striking example, where a purely African concept of African socialism is creating a quite different series of values or criteria for judging the success of a state; here in Tanzania, which ideologically has élite status in Africa, internal élitism is discouraged. At the level of the nation, too, mention has already been made of countries like Burundi with two major groups – the Tutsi, divided into the traditional élite and the politically powerful élite minority – and the Hutu, the serfs, whose own élite was destroyed by the Tutsi. In Uganda we have mentioned the former élitist position of the Baganda and the effect this had on retarding independence in Uganda and in encouraging ethnic conflict and anti-Baganda feelings on the part of the rest of the population. Then the Ewe, as we have seen, live on both sides of the border between Ghana and Togo; and the interesting point here, as far as élitism is concerned, is that in southern Togo the Ewe are the élitist group, whereas in south-eastern Ghana the Ewe are very much on the periphery, both geographically and in their economic, social and political status – a set of circumstances clearly reminiscent of the Catholics in Northern Ireland. One has also to consider the European, or non-indigenous élite groups of Africa – the Indians in East Africa, the Syrians and Lebanese in West Africa, and the whites in southern Africa.

The point has already been made that ethnicity is best seen in urban areas because it is there that the essential ingredient of conflict is present and observable. The same can be said of élitism: that there can be no élitism without conflict or competitive contact. A great deal of work has now been carried out into the study of élitism in many African towns and of the division of the population into relatively homogeneous groups. In Kampala, Ibadan, Lagos, Dakar, Freetown and Kisangani attempts have been made to map and comment on the geographical distribution of these different groups and their associated ethnicity and élitism. The previous section referred to the case of the Hausa and Western Ibo in Ibadan: the Hausa maintained their identity geographically and sociologically, whereas the Western Ibo did not. Cohen goes further and looks at the identity of the Hausa élite group in Ibadan.[16] He draws an analogy with the business élite of the City of London. Here the élite

speak the same language and presumably partake in the same culture of the wider society, but when one looks closely into their style of life one will discover subtle peculiarities – in accent, manner of linguistic expression, style of dress, patterns of friendship and of marriage, etiquette, manners – that are organizationally instrumental in developing boundaries, communication, and other mechanisms for the organization of the group. The élite thus coordinate their corporate activities through their style of life.

The point Cohen is making here is important in Africa because it emphasizes how interest groups try to maintain their identity, not out of purely selfish reasons, but because they cannot otherwise operate effectively in fulfilling their roles.

Transferring this notion to the Hausa, Cohen shows that the Hausa traders act exactly like the City of London men. A Hausa dealer from northern Nigeria will only entrust his money and goods in the south to a Hausa broker; and a Hausa in Ibadan is anxious to preserve the symbols of Hausaism, not only by dressing, speaking and behaving like a Hausa, but also by separating himself physically or residentially from the rest of the population. At independence, however, the Hausa were becoming aware of the danger of being absorbed into the total population. They were particularly affected by party political activities in the city, and by the development of Islamic rituals and ceremonials amongst the indigenous African population. Many of the Yoruba in Ibadan are Moslems and the Hausa were faced with the problem of how to maintain their distinctiveness. The way they did this was simply to adopt a mystical Islamic *sufi* brotherhood called the *Tijanaiya*; this localized the daily rituals, the Hausa no longer prayed with the Yoruba outside the Hausa quarter, and it became necessary for the Hausa to come into the Hausa quarter five times a day to fulfil their religious obligations. The Hausa Islamic community is now therefore a superior, puritanical, ritual community – a religious brotherhood quite distinct from the mass of the Yoruba Moslems in the city. The Hausa now have their own Friday mosque, their own Friday congregation, their own cemetery, and they continue to live quite separately from the rest of the population. Here is an example of how a mechanism is discovered and applied to maintain the separate physical identity of a group of people who feel that their whole economic, physical and spiritual future depends on segregation to maintain their élite status. There are many other examples of the same phenomenon in Africa.

How can we evaluate élitism in Africa? The negative features are considerable and obvious. Élites are socially divisive. Where they are associated with a particular ethnic group they tend to emphasize and reinforce the distinctiveness of the ethnic basis of life and activity, and to reinforce the power of ethnic minorities. Intellectual élites frequently become dangerously alienated from the major practical problems of economic, social and political development – an alienation which is only too apparent in most universities in Africa. Further, in countries where political problems are not yet very manifest, the problem of creating an educated élite with no jobs – unemployed white-collar workers – is becoming acute. On the other hand, the positive functions of élitism cannot be ignored. Élitism can function as a mechanism for modernization, affecting motivation, incentives, linking up within countries and in linking countries together. It is perhaps no accident that the two countries where élitism is perhaps most obvious at the moment are Ivory Coast and Nigeria – the two countries which by conventional western economic criteria are perhaps the most successful. And the country in Africa which is easily the most prosperous in economic terms – South Africa – exhibits a particular form of élitism in the power of the white élite group.

4 Race and reality in southern Africa

It is common to view the problems of southern Africa as a whole and, more especially, to treat the affairs of South Africa and Rhodesia as if they were identical in most important respects. However valid this approach might be, it does tend to cloud some of the particular facts and issues of which we need to be aware and, in any case, the immediate future of the various countries in the region is certain to be so markedly different as to upset any of the more general statements one might otherwise wish to make.

South Africa

There is probably no more emotive issue than race and the apartheid policy in South Africa; it would therefore be naïve to suggest that complete objectivity is possible. But it is probably worth trying to make the attempt. Certainly a great deal of the current discussion reflects a disturbing amount of ignorance about the whole matter. And if the criticisms levelled at South Africa today are to be more effective in bringing about change within that country then they must be more informed, less prejudiced and more realistic. It is also worth remembering that since pre-colonial times Africa has experienced a whole series of successive tyrannies of one form or another, whether of minorities or majorities, and the pre-colonial history of Africa is studded with inter-group wars of often terrifying ferocity and cruelty. Tyranny has been no less a feature of Africa's history than of other parts of the world and it is even a moot point whether apartheid represents the worst form of tyranny in the continent today. Thus the Anti-Slavery Society in London alleges that the government of Equatorial Guinea

> is among the most brutal and unpredictable in the world. The murder and disappearance of most of [the President's] high officials, together with many real or imagined opponents, has caused up to a quarter of the population to seek refuge in other countries . . . [To solve the labour problem, the President has] resorted to criminal compulsion scarcely indistinguishable from slave-raiding and slave-trading.

Similarly, the World Council of Churches and many other bodies allege 'huge and continuing' massacres in Uganda by the present regime there. This is worth saying, not to condone or give support to South Africa's policies, but simply to put the apartheid problem in its true perspective and to question the self-righteous, moral posturing of much contemporary comment.

Apartheid

We have already noted how in 1652 the first Dutch settlement began at the Cape as a revictualling station on the route to the East Indies and that the obvious local opportunities for more permanent settlement and agricultural development were quickly realized. British expansion and administration began in 1806 and the Great Trek eastwards and north-eastwards into the interior by the Dutch Afrikaans took place in the 1830s. After the Boer wars the British granted in 1910 independence to their two colonies (the Cape of Good Hope and Natal) as well as to the republics of Orange Free State and Transvaal, the four territories thereby being united under a constitution creating the Union of South Africa. By this Union, the British placed the administrative responsibility for the entire territory in the hands of the white population of South Africa.

Until after the Second World War, South Africa was administered and planned as one state, but in 1948 the Nationalist Party introduced the notion of physical segregation of the different races – white, Bantu, Indian and Coloured – and for the election of that year coined the word 'apartheid' or 'apartness'. Subsequently, in 1959, the concept was extended to include eventual independence for the Bantu national units and, in the 1960s, re-defined in a more positive way to mean separate development. The then impending independence of Botswana, Lesotho and Swaziland was accepted as simply part of an emergency plan for all of southern Africa. Today, then, emphasis is placed on the multi-national rather than the multi-racial society in South Africa, the official position being that

> our task in South Africa is not primarily that of solving a problem of races, it is a problem of nations, a problem of bringing about a situation where peaceful co-existence of the various nations living in our country will be possible. We believe that this can only be achieved by the independent development of each people towards the full realization of its separate nationhood.

In its simplest terms the policy is as follows. Ten Bantu states, ranged in a discontinuous and fragmented horseshoe around the eastern and north-eastern parts of the Republic, are to become quite separate states and the homelands for some 18,000,000 Bantu in South Africa. Transkei (1976) and Bophuthatswana (1977) have already become independent; the

65

other eight (Venda, Ganzankulu, Lebowa, Ndebele, Savazi, Basotho-Quaqwa, Kwazulu and Ciskei) will move towards independence 'as soon as possible'. The rest of South Africa will continue as at present – a state dominated by some 4,500,000 whites – and in this sense the policy is a kind of bargain: full rights for the Bantu in African areas in return for continued white domination in white areas. As Verwoerd put it in 1961, 'the development of the Bantu states will buy for the white South African his freedom and right to retain domination in his own country, settled for him by his fore-fathers'. In white South Africa the Bantu will continue to have no rights of citizenship or residence. As for the 2,000,000 'Coloureds' and 1,000,000 Indians, these are to be given rights through their own elected councils, though they clearly have no homelands to which they could be directed.

The case for apartheid rests, first, on historical arguments. The Bantu-speaking peoples of South Africa moved into what is now South Africa from the north and north-east at roughly the same time as the whites moved eastwards and north-east-wards from the Cape. Blacks and whites met in the late eighteenth century at the Great Fish river in what is now Eastern Cape Colony. Here a series of clashes – the Kaffir Wars – were abortive in the sense that there were no substantial territorial gains on either side. In 1836 the Great Trek took place into the north-eastern interior plateau, the whites settling in areas which had earlier been settled by Africans but which had more recently been emptied when, in the first decade of the nineteenth century, the *Mfecane* – the expansion of the Zulu Shakai – radically changed the pattern of population distribution. The whole argument, then, suggests that the whites in South Africa never seriously displaced the Bantu and that in general the territorial integrity of the Bantu-speaking peoples has never substantially been infringed. The whites in their own parts of South Africa are therefore no more simply 'settlers' than are the blacks in their own areas.

A second argument is based on the suggestion that the Bantu-speaking peoples constitute distinct national groups with very little in common and often with a good deal of mutual antagonism. Apart from the conflicts between the different ethnic groups, there is today a clear conflict between, on the one hand, those Bantu who refuse to accept the Bantustan policy and are determined to maintain the unity of South Africa and, on the other, the Transkeian authorities who are determined to go ahead with their independent status. There has never been a single black nation in South Africa; it is wrong, therefore, to think of the blacks as any more homogeneous than the whites. The 4,500,000 whites in South Africa are divided roughly between those of English-speaking stock – some 38 per cent of all whites, dating back only to the nineteenth century – and the Afrikaans-speaking group, or some 58 per cent of all whites, dating back to the original Dutch settlers of the seventeenth and eighteenth centuries. Of the white rural population over 80 per cent is Afrikaans, while of the white urban population only 53 per cent is Afrikaans. Furthermore, it is the English-speaking whites who are largely responsible for the rapid modern economic development of the country. The 18,000,000 blacks are divided into several major groups, only two of which (the Xhosa and Zulu) outnumber the white groups numerically. In a sense, therefore, the only common feature of the blacks is their colour. By arrangement in 1910 some of the Bantu national territories came to be administered by the white South African Union, while others – Bechuanaland (now Botswana), Basutoland (now Lesotho) and Swaziland – continued to be ruled by Britain. Both in the three former High Commission territories and in South Africa the separate national identities of the Bantu nations have been respected and they have been prepared for full national independence. In this sense the policy of allocating separate homelands to Bantu nations is no invention of the Nationalist Party. Britain inaugurated it in the High Commission Territories; South Africa is simply continuing that policy.

Thirdly, apartheid is based not on ideology but on pragmatism. To attempt to integrate the various races and societies of South Africa into one single democratic nation is unrealistic and theoretical. Separate development for the whites and blacks in a multi-national country like South Africa flows from the realistic acceptance and recognition of human rights and values. It is not, clearly, a policy for export, but a policy to meet the specific needs and circumstances prevailing in South Africa. The policy of apartheid is not racist in the sense that it assumes the superiority of whites over blacks. Indeed the worst racial riots in recent South African history – in Durban in 1949 – involved the rioting of Africans against Indians. The serious inter-ethnic riots of 1975 provide further evidence of this fact.

Fourthly, it is pointed out that the material standards of living of Africans in South Africa are probably higher than anywhere else to the north of the Republic, and peace and security are, by African standards, well established. In housing, health, education and economic opportunities the African in South Africa is infinitely better off than is his counterpart to the north. Indeed, this is one reason why there are probably not less than 1,000,000 immigrants (many of them illegal) from other countries now working in South Africa. Anti-white activities north of the Zambezi have little to do with genuine concern for the Bantu people of South Africa. It is significant that it is those African countries where steady progress in the economic field has been a feature of independence (for example Ivory Coast) which have taken the lead in establishing a dialogue between black Africa and white South Africa.

A fifth argument emphasizes that apartheid is designed to protect the standards of living and rights of whites in their own national territory. For most whites, South Africa is their own country, often for generations back, and they have no other national home; for the Afrikaaner, more particularly, this is a vital principle – that he is a member of a separate *volk*. It is pointed out that Afrikaaner nationalism precipitated the first anti-colonial wars in Africa, namely the Anglo-Boer wars of 1880–1 and 1899–1902. Moreover, Afrikaaners claim to be ethnically indigenous in Africa – the only truly 'white nation' on the continent. They note that theirs is the only language containing in its name the name of the continent.

Finally, true apartheid is not to be identified with 'petty' or 'negative' apartheid. 'Petty' apartheid refers to separate schools, residential areas, buses, taxis, train coaches, hospitals and so on, and the current policy of the South African government is progressively to reduce and eventually to abolish these irritants. The town council of Krugersdorp (Transvaal) became in 1974 the first municipal body dominated by the Nationalist Party to take steps to abandon offensive petty apartheid regulations, and since then many other councils have followed this example. True apartheid, on the other hand, refers to the more fundamental and long-term basis of the policy: a dynamic and adaptable policy in which each nation is free to develop its independence in its own way. The emergence of the fully independent state of Transkei during 1976 is proof of the dynamic nature of apartheid as a policy aimed at granting complete independence to all the Bantustan nations.

The case against apartheid begins with a rather different interpretation of the facts of history. It is argued that whites *did* indeed displace many Hottentot and Bushmen, as well as large numbers of Bantu. In the east the whites are known to have bartered and bought land from the Bantu. But, more importantly, the fact that there were only a few Bantu in the area when whites first moved into the north-eastern interior is irrelevant and reveals a basic misunderstanding of the African's attitude to land – that one did not need to 'occupy' land continuously in order to 'own' it and, indeed, that the very concept of land 'ownership' was at that time meaningless to Africans.

Secondly, the Bantu homelands constitute only 13·7 per cent of the total land area of South Africa. The homelands are already overcrowded and if the 10,000,000 or so Bantu now living in the white, largely urban, areas of South Africa went to join the 8,000,000 Bantu left in the homelands then conditions there would become insupportable: soil erosion, poverty and over-grazing are already widespread. In spite of the 1956 Tomlinson Commission's report, development in the Bantu homelands has been slow – in terms of job creation only about one-tenth of what was planned – and, in spite of the Border Industries Policy and the Bantu Investment Corporation, relatively little industry has yet benefited the Bantu homelands.

Moreover, these homelands are highly fragmented into numerous (113) non-contiguous pieces. In other words, these embryonic black states do not satisfy the minimum requirements for economic viability and thus lack the ingredient without which a state cannot hope to exist.

Thirdly, it is argued that apartheid is basically an expression of racialism – the belief that there are superior (white) and inferior (black) peoples. Such a belief is both scientifically baseless and morally reprehensible. The real purpose of apartheid, so it is argued, is simply to maintain white supremacy. The kind of prejudice exhibited in 'petty' or 'negative' apartheid, which affronts the dignity of Africans, is clear evidence of this. For this reason, and because the great wealth of white South Africa has been built up very largely with black labour, the non-whites do not want a Balkanized sub-continent. They want to share in the wealth they have helped to create and reject any policy which attempts to break up South Africa. So far, black South Africans have benefited directly only to a limited extent in economic terms from the country's growing prosperity. The *per capita* income in 1973 for South Africa was US$1,200, putting South Africa about thirty-fifth in the World Bank's league table. But since 4,500,000 whites take some three-quarters of the national income while 20,000,000 non-whites share the remainder, this leaves white South African incomes about twelve times those of black Africans. Moreover, the gap between white and black incomes is still growing. The fact that Africans in South Africa are substantially better off materially than Africans in countries to the north is irrelevant; it would be surprising if Africans in South Africa were not materially better off than in other parts of Africa, considering the much greater mineral wealth of South Africa. The only valid comparison is with the standards of living of whites in South Africa.

Fourthly, apartheid cannot deal with the 2,000,000 Coloureds (mixed Bantu, Hottentot, Negroid slaves, Europeans and Bushmen) and 1,000,000 Indians (imported originally as indentured labourers for the Natal sugar estates). There is no place to which these two important groups can be sent. The concept of a nation cannot therefore be applied territorially to the Coloureds and Indians. These groups must be politically and economically integrated into the Republic. They cannot remain in the no-man's land between the blacks and whites. There is no question of the Coloureds or Indians merging with the Bantu. While Coloureds deplore the distinction between them and the whites, they draw a very rigid line between themselves and the Bantu.

Fifthly, it is impossible to conceive of the 10,000,000 Bantu – over half the total Bantu in South Africa – who now live in the white areas returning in any significant numbers to the Bantustans or homelands. This 10,000,000 constitutes the vast, urbanized African proletariat which is economically integrated into the white areas. These Africans cannot and do not want to go back to their homelands, and the South African economy cannot afford that they should do so. All attempts to stop the flow of Bantu to white areas have so far failed; indeed, in the two decades of Nationalist rule the number of Africans in the white areas has risen from 2,000,000 to 10,000,000. It is clearly impossible to eliminate the economic and social forces now on the move in South African society. Economic integration of blacks in the white areas is deep-rooted and irrevocable. The non-white population in 'white' South Africa is there to stay. That this is now a fact has been recognized in the agreement between the South African government and the authorities of the Transkei, which achieved independence in 1976. All Xhosa with residence in Transkei are to be Transkeians, together with those born there and merely on short contracts to work in the Republic; but the mass of urban Xhosa, or those long domiciled in the black townships and farms of South Africa, are to remain South Africa's responsibility. This agreement at one stroke destroys the theory of separate development.

External relations

It is of course true that the root of the problem of potential conflict in South Africa is wholly indigenous in that it derives from the blacks' determination to get rid of the white supremacist regime there, as in other parts of southern Africa. But the problems faced by the South African government at home are immensely compounded by external forces and pressures, not only within Africa but throughout the world. It will be necessary to develop this point further in the final chapter, but a few preliminary comments seem necessary here. In the immediate post-war period, and after the accession of the Nationalist government in 1948, the racial element in the government's policy was for many observers associated with Nazi sentiments, the white-dominated government was associated with colonialism, and South Africa's refusal to give up the trusteeship territory of South-West Africa was taken as final proof of the essentially racist and colonial nature of the South African government's policy. The interaction of external and internal factors was by now clear:

the external factors have included the heightened consciousness, particularly in the Western world (and reflected in the United Nations Charter), of human rights as an issue affecting international relations; the anti-colonial movement, particularly as expressed in the achievement of independence throughout Africa; and the cold war conflict between the Western and Communist powers. The inability of South Africa's internal political system to adapt adequately to these far-reaching changes in the post-war world caused a progressive deterioration in its external relations, resulting in increasing international isolation on a political level.[17]

In 1960 the Sharpeville shootings were interpreted by the United Nations as a 'threat to world peace'. South Africa was forced to withdraw from several United Nations agencies – from ILO, FAO, CTTA, CSA and ECA; and in 1961, when South Africa became a Republic, it withdrew from the Commonwealth. Thus by the early 1960s South Africa was isolated and forced to look inwards in a hostile world.

The two main effects of this enforced isolation were predictable. Defensive attitudes developed and the threat of sanctions, external criticisms and the general isolation welded the white communities together in a manner that would perhaps never have occurred otherwise. Secondly, South Africa began rapidly to build up its own military strength and economic independence, for example in oil. But then the Simonstown agreement of 1965 passed almost without comment, and in 1966 the International Court gave its judgement on South-West Africa in favour of South Africa. Suddenly the threats from outside seemed less pressing. South Africa was now strong and her control of South-West Africa had been legalized. Indeed, until the withdrawal of the Portuguese from Angola and Mozambique in 1975 South Africa seemed to be becoming increasingly confident in the world. Within Africa it was having some considerable success in its efforts to encourage dialogue rather than confrontation or isolation. As the president of the Ivory Coast put it, 'to solve the problem of South Africa negotiation is necessary, not force. For seven years we have had nothing but grand and violent speeches, with tragic and sometimes ridiculous results. We cannot make threats without the means to apply them'. And in Malawi, Banda has followed a pragmatic policy in foreign affairs, facing the realities of the country's position *vis-à-vis* South Africa and negotiating with rather than confronting the South African government. Now, however, Malawi can be considered to be a prisoner of the Marxist FRELIMO government of Mozambique and has become much more vulnerable to attack by opponents based in Tanzania. Malawi's experiment in dialogue seems likely to be at an end. Other countries, like Liberia, Malagasy, Gabon, Benin and Central African Empire, have also been following a similar line in the past though they have recently withdrawn from what they call the 'dialogue situation'. These contacts have been significant because, unlike Lesotho, Botswana and Swaziland, these 'negotiating' countries do not abut directly on to South African territory. The former High Commission territories are not only adjacent to or in South Africa but are also landlocked. All three, in fact, are in a monetary and customs union with South Africa. The Lusaka Manifesto of 1969, on the other hand, reflects the policy of Kaunda and Nyerere – a policy of confrontation with South Africa and support for liberation movements. This policy, which has

73

recently begun to seem much more practical and widely supported, has gained ground and stimulus from the success of the Russian-backed Cuban forces in Angola. What South Africa's relations with independent Angola and Mozambique become remains to be seen.

The two polarized views of the South African situation today are represented by complete apartheid – in which Bantu homelands eventually become independent – and complete integration of all races within the present boundaries of the country, meaning black majority rule. The first of these is the stated policy of the Afrikaans-dominated National Party. In recent years support for the National Party has grown to include many English-speaking South Africans, especially as a result of the resurgence of international criticism of apartheid. At the 1977 general election it swept back into power with a substantially increased majority, winning 81 per cent of the seats as against 72 per cent in the previous general election. The National Party is now immensely strong. The moderate United Party, formerly the main white opposition party, is now extinct; its policy was holistic, following Smuts' views and the dictum that 'the central idea of secession is the essence of anarchy'. The United Party was therefore concerned to maintain the geographical unity of South Africa and argued that each community or ethnic group should have its own council which would consult with the central authority. The Progressive Federal Party, now the main opposition party, has had some recent increase in support. This party goes much further than the old United Party and argues for a policy leading to a multiracial society in South Africa. All South Africans, of whatever colour, would be given the vote over the age of eighteen as long as they also possessed certain not over-stringent educational or economic qualifications; majority black rule would quickly follow in the new state of 'Azania'. Should the PFP be able to attract other white parties and present a united opposition to the Nationalist Party, then such a combination might reach some accommodation with the non-enfranchised black parties in South Africa. And could a mass black party capable of responding in parallel be created, then some real dialogue

74

might indeed take place. The new Black United Front Party attempts to link moderate black opinion in the black townships of white South Africa with developments in the homelands.

The crux of the whole problem lies in the existence of over half of the Bantu in white areas where economic integration has already occurred to the mutual benefit of both blacks and whites. The South African government has never begun to resolve the inherent contradictions between its economic and political objectives; and the rapidly developing unrest in the black townships since the Soweto riots of June 1976 are but one indication of this. The fundamental dilemma of white South Africans is that they cannot achieve their objective of continued and rapid economic growth without endangering the social and racial fabric to which they attach such value. As a simple fact, the two communities are mutually dependent in a way that whites and blacks further north in Africa never were, and the problems of neither can be solved by the removal or permanent frustration of the other. This central issue must also be seen in the context of South Africa's great wealth and still resilient economy. In its dealings with South Africa the outside world cannot forget that with only 6 per cent of Africa's population South Africa accounts for 25 per cent of the continent's GNP, 90 per cent of the steel production and 63 per cent of the electricity produced in Africa. Whereas in most of Africa real income per head is rising at no more than 1 per cent per annum, if at all, in South Africa the rate is at least three and a half times that figure.

It is tempting to consider possible compromise proposals. One might, for instance, suggest a consolidation of the discontinuous horseshoe pattern of Bantu homelands, giving the eastern section a substantial and continuous seaboard. Such a division would give Africans a country of a size, location, population and resources that would appear to offer some reasonable viability for an independent state. Africans would then possess an even larger part of the higher rainfall areas of South Africa. Only a quarter of South Africa has over 25 inches of rainfall a year, 65 per cent has less than 15 inches a year, and 30 per cent has less than 10 inches a year. The argument so often advanced against apartheid – that 13·7 per cent of the land area is meant to support some 80 per cent of the total population – has never had much geographical validity. Even today, over 45 per cent of the most fertile and best-watered land in South Africa lies within existing Bantu homelands. And although such a plan of consolidation and extension of the Bantu homelands would mean the whites giving up large areas, including the Durban area, they would still control not only the maize triangle but also the industrial heart of the Republic – the Pretoria–Witwatersrand–Vereeniging zone – which contains one-fifth of South Africa's total population and one-third of all whites and generates 36 per cent of the country's national production. Investment in the new Bantu territory would have to be large and immediate, designed to encourage the Bantu back to develop their land and economy; it would also have to encourage industrial/urban growth as well as purely agricultural development. But there would be no compulsion. If a Bantu wished to remain in white South Africa he would have to wait until he possessed sufficient educational and/or economic qualifications before becoming enfranchised. In practice, as indeed is already happening, the colour bar would weaken, the African middle class would strengthen, and the possibilities of true integration would become less remote.

Such a compromise solution might until recently have been acceptable, in view of the rapidly deteriorating situation along South Africa's northern borders and bordering states; there is also the internal demographic situation in which differential rates of natural increase (3·5 per cent per annum for the blacks, and likely to increase as health measures improve further) are producing a changing proportion of whites to non-whites in South Africa – from 1:3·6 in 1921 to 1:5 today and likely to be 1:8 by the end of the century. But the chances are that it is too late for such a compromise to be accepted by Africans and that the only practical solution now is rapid progress towards full integration and black majority rule. At this late stage it is perhaps naïve even to hope that change will be evolutionary rather than revolutionary. Military logistics, the intensity of the interest of the rest of Africa and the outside world in South

Africa, and the large number of whites in the country – all these factors suggest that revolutionary change would initially be at the expense of the black population of South Africa, though the success of terrorist groups in Mozambique, of the MPLA in Angola and, more distantly, the result of the Vietnam struggle, have given Africans the confidence to consider seriously such guerrilla activities as a means to political ends in a way that was inconceivable only a few years ago. The future of South Africa must also depend to a great extent upon how quickly and smoothly the inevitable transfer to majority rule in Rhodesia takes place, and upon the degree of success achieved by independent Transkei in dealing with her own social, especially ethnic, and economic problems. Nevertheless, the dangers to the Bantu of armed revolution in South Africa are real and are well recognized by responsible African leaders in the country; in general they are not calling for the 'expulsion' or 'extermination' of whites in South Africa; and the essential interdependence of all races is, at least ostensibly, the basis of even the most extreme African or liberal views in the country.

It is true that there are signs of the South African government facing up to the immediate dangers of the apartheid policy as rapidly as internal white political conditions allow. Apart from the reduction in petty apartheid already referred to, some of the racially more harsh and discriminatory measures against black urban Africans have been relaxed. Blacks outside their homelands have now been granted self-government up to town council level, and leasehold rights to their homes. The Asiatic and Coloured groups now have their own legislative councils and have recently formed a consultative 'cabinet committee' together with government ministers; this is seen as a possible forerunner to a federal form of multi-racial government. Moreover the 10 black 'homelands' are soon to be given their independence; Transkei is to be followed by Bophutatswana, Venda and Ciskei; and consolidation of the 113 fragments into 36 units is planned. The world is to be faced with separate development and the existence of independent Bantustans as a fact.

77

Several of the homeland leaders are opposed to independence on the present terms, however. As Legum has put it,

> the future of South Africa's policy of 'separate development' depends on whether the partition of the republic into one state embracing two-thirds of the country, and ten black states sharing the rest, will offer an acceptable basis for a peaceful settlement between 18 million Africans and 4 million whites.[18]

Put in this way, no such solution is likely. Added to this, Transkei's 'independence' is still not recognized and is unlikely to be recognized by any African government outside South Africa, and to this extent the whole Bantustan policy is doomed to failure.

In the end, whatever solution is found will be of worldwide significance. Perhaps it is no longer a matter of whether apartheid is good or bad, right or wrong, moral or immoral, justified or unjustified: its immediate future is more secure than it ever was. And South Africa's strategic position in relation to the Atlantic and Indian Oceans, her mineral resources and the enormous size of western investment in South Africa (40 per cent of its industry is foreign-owned) – all are vital ingredients in the interest shown by the outside world in South African affairs. Whatever the local moral arguments of the case, the western world cannot afford to allow South Africa to lapse into chaos. This, in the final analysis, might prove to be the real imperative.

South-West Africa (Namibia)

The problem of South-West Africa is part of the problem of South Africa. It will be remembered that South-West Africa, German territory until 1914, was a mandate and later trusteeship territory of the United Nations, administered by South Africa. For all practical purposes, however, South-West Africa was fully integrated into the South African economy. The movement for independence in the territory received something of a setback when the International Court at The Hague ruled in South Africa's favour concerning the legitimacy of her continuing control of South-West Africa. Subsequently, however, the independence movement gathered momentum, and South African plans for Bantustans – Ovambo and Kavango – were scrapped. Most recently, the South African government has agreed to grant full independence to South-West Africa within the next two years, but has refused to negotiate with the external wing of SWAPO (South-West Africa Peoples Organization) and, to this extent, the proposed independence of the territory is considered by African opinion, especially in the OAU, to be neither legitimate nor complete. From South Africa's point of view, her position is justified since there is one fundamental difference between the internal and external wings of SWAPO – the internal wing is opposed to violence whereas the external wing is committed to liberation through armed struggle.

A resolution calling for 'armed struggle' to end Pretoria's control of South-West Africa was accepted by the United Nations General Assembly in January 1977, thereby condoning the use of violent solutions to Africa's problems. Perhaps this represents a recognition of the fact that it is now too late for compromise solutions. The United Nations had earlier recognized SWAPO as the 'sole' representative of the Namibia people, though SWAPO began by representing only the Ovambo ethnic faction (albeit the best organized politically and militarily) in the country. In South-West Africa there are eleven identifiable ethnic groups of varying population size. The whites (some 100,000) form the second largest group after the Ovambo, who comprise about 46 per cent of the total population of rather over 850,000. They live – and this of course is another consideration in South Africa's attitude – in northern South-West Africa bordering on Angola.

What happens in South-West Africa is of immense significance to South Africa. If, as South Africa fears, SWAPO gains complete control of the territory, then the communist, largely Soviet, presence would be extended down from Angola to South Africa's borders and, through the Caprivi Strip, up to the Zambezi and Rhodesia.

Rhodesia (Zimbabwe)

The facts of the Rhodesian situation are now all too well known. In a country only half as large again as England live some 272,000 whites (largely of British stock) and 6,400,000 Africans – a ratio, that is, of 1:24. Refusing to accept the principle of eventual majority rule in Rhodesia, the white minority government announced in 1965 a Unilateral Declaration of Independence (UDI). The United Nations imposed economic sanctions on Rhodesia, but the economy of the country was not seriously affected, due partly to the support given to Rhodesia by South Africa and others, and partly to the existence of the weak flanking territories of Portuguese Mozambique to the east and independent Botswana to the west. While the *status quo* could be maintained Rhodesia was a key link in the group of 'buffer states' lying to the north of the 'white redoubt' of South Africa. Until the withdrawal of Portugal from Mozambique, the position of this whole buffer zone seemed to be reasonably secure for some time to come.

Now, however, all is changed. Rhodesia faces pressure from Zambia in the north, Mozambique in the east and from Botswana in the west. And in the south, South Africa – now Rhodesia's only outlet to the sea – seems content to see a black majority government and so some kind of stability in Rhodesia; the alternative would be a rapid escalation of terrorism within Rhodesia and along its borders and the eventual collapse of the Rhodesian white regime. Rhodesia, like South Africa, must immediately face the realities of her position. It is not now a matter of whether black majority rule is desirable, wise or necessary; it is not now even a matter of morality, pragmatism or anything else. The fact is that black majority rule in Rhodesia is now inevitable, and the current 'negotiations' can only affect, if at all, the timing and method of transition to black majority rule; they certainly cannot affect the final outcome.

It is possible to argue that Rhodesian politics are at bottom the politics of land. The present race laws carve up the land so that the whites and blacks each have one-half of the land area of the country. The white Rhodesian Front Party is controlled by the farmers, whose assets are considerable and immovable, whereas the independence movement is basically a movement for black peasant proprietorship or cooperatives. Thus land purchase is the only offer of substance which the British government can make to change the last-ditch attitude of Rhodesian farmers: 'land purchase has been the historic and successful agent of British decolonization in areas containing substantial minorities hostile to independence'.[19] Kenya is frequently cited as the best recent example in Africa of how this land problem can be solved. According to one common interpretation, the white farmers in Rhodesia could not reasonably expect a more orderly, satisfactory or successful transition than their counterparts have experienced in Kenya. Although, admittedly, the pattern of farming is different in Rhodesia, there are clear lessons to be learned from the Kenya Land Transfer Programme. Over 1,000 British-owned farms have changed hands since the Land Transfer Programme began and fewer than 100 white farmers left Kenya. Nearly 70,000 African settlers have become land-owners. Other interpretations, however, focus on the 'iniquities' of the Kenyan programme and emphasize the differences between the Kenyan and Rhodesian land problems. Here, as in so many other spheres, the same facts are given different interpretations according to the use to be made of them.

It is, indeed, difficult to avoid the conclusion that Rhodesian politics are at bottom not the politics of land but rather the politics of fear, prejudice, survival and above all of power. As one line of argument goes, we must, in judging the Rhodesian issue, 'get off the various post-colonial, ideological, kith and kin or negrophile hooks on which we are impaled, and judge the problem in the simpler and more brutal terms of power politics'.[20]

African opinion in Rhodesia is by no means solid: Africans are not agreed on the kind of power or black control they wish to see; nor are they agreed on the methods to be used to attain that control. The political, ideological conflict is underlain by the long-standing ethnic differences among black Rhodesians; the whites in Rhodesia are always emphasizing the ethnic antagonisms between, more especially, the Matabele and the more numerous, but less bellicose, Mashona. The two main guerrilla movements – ZANU (led by Mugabe, a Shona) and ZAPU (led by Nkomo, a Matabele) – have now been united in the Patriotic Front nationalist alliance, which is backed by Soviet Russia, the OAU and the so-called five 'Front-line Presidents' of Tanzania, Zambia, Mozambique, Botswana and Angola. The two other nationalist figures — Muzorewa and Sithole – appear to have been largely isolated from the Patriotic Front alliance, even though it is believed that the vast majority of black Rhodesians support the Muzorewa/Sithole factions. Yet white Rhodesians cannot derive any satisfaction, yet alone hope, from this fact. For all black opinion is at least united in its determination to see the end of the white minority regime in Salisbury; and any conflict between the various African factions is likely to post-date the demise of the present government of Rhodesia. The most recent attempts to relax the race laws, including those relating to land ownership, and to reach an internal settlement in Rhodesia, are unlikely to have any success, being both too small and too late.

There are so many uncertainties that it is futile to speculate too much about the Rhodesian problem. But it is clear, as the South African government itself recognizes, that black rule in Rhodesia is both inevitable and necessary. It is the way in which black rule comes about and the nature of that rule that will deeply, perhaps decisively, affect what happens subsequently in the Republic of South Africa. The signs are not hopeful The present (1977) attempt by Smith to negotiate an internal settlement with the black leaders inside Rhodesia on the basis of an agreed, orderly and secure transfer to black majority rule may be both sincere and, within its limits, successful. But no such attempt can have any lasting success unless it includes in all discussions the leaders of the externally based Patriotic Front alliance, supported as it is by powerful external forces. The Rhodesian issue is, perhaps unfortunately, no longer a simple internal problem capable of an internal solution. Britain, the United States, Russia and China are all, in their various ways and for their various reasons, concerned to influence the direction events take in Rhodesia; and the Patriotic Front alliance clearly takes much comfort, not only from these conflicting forces of interest, but also, and quite explicitly, from the success of the Vietnamese in what, so it is claimed, was an analogous situation in south-east Asia. Certainly the Patriotic Front cannot support any kind of democratic election in Rhodesia at the moment. Here in Rhodesia, it seems likely that whatever happens in the immediate future – in the promotion of black majority rule through an internal settlement – white minority rule will eventually be replaced by black minority rule.

The issues of South Africa, Rhodesia and South-West Africa are related in many fundamental ways, but this relationship is perhaps most crucial in the sense that the two issues of Rhodesia and South-West Africa represent for Africans the last vestiges of colonialism, with South Africa in effect playing the role of the colonial power. It is for this reason, as suggested in the present chapter, that black majority rule for the whole of southern Africa is inevitable. But for the black southern African, majority rule will not be the end of his problems, any more than independence has been for Africans elsewhere in the continent. All must ultimately face the much more difficult and intractable problems of economic, social and political development. The countries of southern Africa are interlinked and interdependent in a way that is only just becoming critically apparent. More especially, the black countries have not ended their dependence on the white economies for food. In a bad year all of them except Malawi need to import food-stuffs, especially maize from Rhodesia or South Africa. Kaunda has recently proclaimed that Zambia must now make agriculture its leading industry, not only because of the troubles with copper – international controls on production, prices and problems of delivery – but also because of Zambia's desperate food dependency on non-Africans. In the 1960s Kaunda's policy was to buy out the white farmers in conformity with the policy of 'Africanization'. But now the remaining white ('commercial') farms are given priority, for some 450 of them produce 40 per cent of the nation's food. Mozambique, too, is heavily dependent on Rhodesia and South Africa for maize. It may be that this dependency on 'white food' is partly the result of the draining-off of a large part of the most effective manpower into South Africa or, in Zambia's case, of too great an emphasis on the industrial/urban sector. But such are the economic realities which could make nonsense of political rhetoric.

5 The economic basis of national development

The importance of economic or material progress, however defined, to social and political stability and so ultimately to the whole question of national unity and independence in African countries will already be apparent from the preceding chapters. In almost all cases, the economic basis has still to be built. Africa is full of countries where real living standards are not perceptibly improving for the majority of the population, where social and political developments are frustrated by poverty, and where the rhetoric of politics and economic planning contrasts vividly with the reality of economic failure. It is not too much to suggest that many of the coups, counter-coups and military governments in Africa have their origin in the failure of successive governments to provide even the beginnings of economic and material progress.

However one defines development – and for the purposes of the present discussion we may take as an *ad hoc* definition 'the process which results in a perceptible and cumulative rise in the standard of living for an increasing proportion of a population' – one does not have to be a pessimist to suggest that the economic basis of most African states is very weak indeed, and that their economic performance is bad. Of the 29 countries defined by UNCTAD as 'least developed countries', 18 are from Africa; and the lack of ability on the part of Africa to withstand events such as the oil crisis since the mid-1970s is shown by the fact that of the 32 countries designated by the United Nations as 'the most seriously affected by the oil crisis', 20 are from Africa. Even those few states with relatively high *per capita* incomes do not strike one as 'developing' in the sense accepted above; the majority of the population is experiencing no real improvement in its standards of living, material prosperity or economic opportunities. Inefficient or non-existent telephone, telegraph and postal services; inadequate and poorly maintained roads, even in the main towns; appalling traffic congestion and chaos in the cities; poor or non-existent sanitation; large and inefficient bureaucracies; incivility and corruption at all levels – this is the picture of which visitors to most African countries are only too aware. Reports of inquiries into bribery and corruption are common features of the African scene, and one report in Ghana in 1975 concluded, as have many similar reports elsewhere, that corruption is 'endemic throughout the whole society'. But these are really only the superficial expressions of a deeply rooted economic stagnation and failure, in both rural and urban areas. Furthermore, it is sometimes difficult to avoid the conclusion that the current emphasis by governments and the largely government-controlled press on corruption is simply one way of distracting people's attention from the serious and fundamental failures of governments to stimulate economic growth.

The social and political implications of the failure of independent African states to 'develop' are potentially frightening. African states seem to be experiencing the evils rather than the benefits of 'development', and to this extent the scenarios are probably being set for radical, revolutionary change by the urban proletariat, rural poor or disillusioned middle classes.

On the one hand there are states like Tanzania, with a strong African socialist ideology, determined to create a self-reliant economy, to break away from neo-colonial dependency, and to spread the benefits of development more evenly, both spatially and structurally, within Tanzanian society. The reality, however, is that Tanzania remains by any criteria one of the poorest states, and faces the danger that her admirable and widely admired plans for social and political development will founder on the rock of economic failure. Tanzania is facing growing economic difficulties which appear all the more serious when compared with the relative progress in achieving higher material standards of living across the border in Kenya. Tanzania's 'operation *maduka*', designed to take over shops previously owned by Asians or Arabs, has been a failure as, to some extent, has been the Tanzanian government's campaign to settle the population in community villages.

On the other hand there is Nigeria, with its new-found and vast wealth from oil, making her seventh among the world OPEC countries and certainly the wealthiest of the black African nations, pursuing a largely western capitalistic line of development; and although in terms of investment, trade and general commercial activity the country is wealthy by African standards, there is little sense of 'development' in the country; little social modernization, economic viability or political stability seems to be emerging, and the vast majority of Nigerians, both rural and urban, do not seem as yet to be benefiting 'perceptibly and cumulatively' from this wealth. In both these cases, the stated aims of development are clearly not being achieved and the gap between the rhetoric and reality of development grows daily wider. Yet there is no doubt that all African governments are only too aware of the importance of economic success, however one defines it, as a *sine qua non* of social and political stability and so of their survival as independent nations. The determination to break out of poverty into material prosperity was always an important and sometimes a decisive motive in the drive for political independence. But just as surely, no independent African nation can expect a sustained period of political stability unless at the same time effective economic development takes place and its benefits are passed on to the bulk of the population. Once generated, the 'revolution of rising expectations' cannot be ignored with impunity.

Why should the economic performance of African countries since independence be so poor? Why is it difficult to point to any country in Africa where the economic basis for social and political progress can yet be said to exist? It is of course impossible to give any adequate answer to this question in one short chapter. But it is a question that must be asked, for all the issues in African affairs with which we are concerned here, however ostensibly political, socio-political or even psychological they may appear, have their roots firmly planted in economic failure.

To many observers, of course, the first, most important, and even the only answer lies in the continuing neo-colonial dependency of most African countries. As with many parts of the developing world, African economies still depend on what has been called the colonial pattern of trade; their prosperity is excessively dependent on the export of a few primary products – mostly minerals and agricultural produce – and they are obliged to import most of the manufactured goods they require. The terms of trade for African countries have been fluctuating wildly since the early 1960s. Their economies are subjected to damaging movements in the world prices or demand for a very limited number of products and there are virtually no established overseas markets for such manufactured goods as African countries do produce. There is a pressing need for developing African countries to gain effective access to existing channels of world trade, but even then there remains the difficulty that many African states are suspicious of trading agreements on the grounds that they represent a form of neo-colonialism.

Europeans, then, 'underdeveloped Africa' and are, together with other western and eastern powers, through aid, trade, and investment, playing the same role in Africa today. The dualistic colonial economies still persist and, while they persist, they must inhibit true economic progress or independence. Economic development and so political stability can come only if Africa can disengage from its exploitative, dependent relationship with the industrialized nations. More will be said about this point of view later, but it is important to recognize that there is a substantial body of opinion, both within and outside Africa, which accepts this diagnosis of what is wrong with African economic development. It is therefore an important point of view to consider, as it emphasizes that social and political progress is determined not so much by economic failure or progress but rather the reverse – that an economy's failure or success is itself caused by the social and political system within which it has to operate, and that the only effective answer to economic failure is to change that social and political context. Those who follow this line of argument point to the typically 'western' competition for power and wealth in a country like Nigeria, to what is termed the 'colonial and class-ridden structure of Nigerian society' and to the conspicuous expenditure on non-productive goods and activities in the country.

Other writers take a very different, largely physically deterministic approach in attempting to answer this question. In particular, lack of water and poverty of soils are said to set fundamental limitations on African development and are put forward as the main reason why Africa is so little developed today. Certainly in this most tropical of continents moisture is more often a limiting factor to plant growth than is temperature. Dry climates are more extensive in Africa, which contains about a third of the world's deserts and semi-deserts, than in any other continent. Not only is there inadequate precipitation, but much of Africa suffers also from great fluctuations of rainfall within individual seasons and from year to year: the great African Sahelian Drought catastrophe of the 1972–4 period is recent and eloquent testimony to this fact. It is true, also, that many African soils, especially those that are heavily leached, suffer from very poor nutrient status and structure, and that there are proportionately fewer young and fertile alluvial soils than in other continents. Soil erosion, too, has become a serious problem in some areas. A further disadvantage in the natural resource base of most African countries is said to be the low economic value of the vegetation, much of which has been degraded by centuries of burning, grazing and shifting cultivation. Even much of the so-called rainforest cover is in fact forest-savanna woodland, whose trees are not generally suitable for lumbering. Many of the savanna grasses, also, have only a low nutritive value for domestic livestock.

Admittedly there are problems of the physical environment which present certain constraints on economic development in African countries, but it is to be doubted whether they raise really insuperable barriers. It is easy to exaggerate them, forgetting that most indigenous agricultural systems show remarkably successful adaptations to physical limitations. If the empirically acquired skills of traditional African agriculture can be successively combined with modern techniques of water conservation and soil improvement these deficiencies can be largely overcome and productivity greatly increased. Moreover, there is much in the physical environment of the continent that is clearly advantageous for economic development.

Most important, perhaps, is the wealth of water power and the presence of minerals, including oil and fissionable raw materials. Africa's water power resources are thought to exceed 40 per cent of the world's potential, about 18 per cent of which is to be found in the Congo river basin alone. While the usefulness of the great rivers of Africa – the Nile, Zambezi, Limpopo, Orange, Zaïre and Niger – as routes of transport is severely restricted by the cataracts and gorges along their lower courses, these and many lesser rivers have for this very reason a high potential use for reservoir construction and hydroelectric power generation. The production of petroleum and natural gas is increasing rapidly, especially in Libya and Nigeria, as well as in Gabon and Angola (Cabinda). The deposits of fissionable material in Zaïre include rich uranium ores and are matched by other fissionable material in Nigeria, Zambia, Mozambique and Gabon. Africa is also a storehouse of non-energy-producing minerals – bauxite, chrome, cobalt, copper, diamonds, gold, iron, manganese, niobium, phosphates, platinum and tantalum – but in almost all cases the importance of mineral deposits to Africa is for export, and so as a means of earning foreign exchange. Nevertheless, the material base for substantial industrial development in Africa certainly exists, though much has still to be done in the way of geological survey and topographical mapping.

A third line of thinking on the question of why Africa's economic performance is so poor raises the whole issue of the human resources of the continent, considered both quantitatively and qualitatively. Quantitatively, consideration is given to the large number of states and very small populations of many African countries; it is argued that over much of Africa densities are too low and that there are too few people in most countries to provide an adequately large domestic market or labour supply for rapid economic advance. How, it is argued, can a country like Gambia with only 500,000 people, or Togo with only 2,000,000, provide the necessary domestic market or labour supply for rapid industrial development? On the other hand, some writers see over-population as the major problem in certain restricted areas and emphasize the present high rates of natural increase (now averaging about 2·5 per cent per annum) as severely limiting in that the benefits of economic development are dissipated by rapid population growth. Furthermore, this rate of natural increase can only rise still further in the foreseeable future as death rates are brought down more quickly than birth rates.

Emphasis is also commonly placed on the quality of Africa's human resources; and here it is important to recognize the fact that many observers do seriously believe, though they may not always admit it, that Africans do not have the capacity for rapid and sustained economic advance in the modern world; that Africans are, in this sense, innately 'inferior' human types, and that sometimes, indeed, they are also corrupt, unreliable and lazy. Other writers argue that the enervating tropical climate over much of Africa is such as to produce peoples who are disinclined to work hard and are both physically and mentally incapable of sustained effort. Such beliefs – unscientific, inaccurate and prejudiced though they are – are nevertheless implicit in much of the discussion on African affairs, and it is to miss one of the main sources of error and mis-understanding to pretend otherwise.

But to take a sentimental, negrophile view is equally danger-ous and misleading. The real point is that the human resources of Africa *are* often poor or inadequate, but this is not because of any inherent characteristics but simply because Africans still suffer under a huge weight of disabilities which have long been removed in most other parts of the world. Without labouring this point, it is worth noting that the generally low standards of health and education in African countries do very seriously inhibit economic, social and political progress. The endemic diseases – malaria, sleeping sickness and many de-ficiency and intestinal diseases – sap energy, reduce initiative and lower efficiency. Lack of education – probably two-thirds of the African population is still illiterate – is an inhibiting factor almost everywhere. Again, there is much in the nature of African ethnicity and social structure which makes any rapid adaptation to modern economic activity peculiarly difficult. Yet however true it is that the attitudes and characteristics of Africans are medically, educationally and socio-culturally deter-mined, the fact remains that most Africans do not seem – at least to European observers – to display the drive, sustained hard work, self-discipline and thrusting economic ambition conventionally associated with successful economic perform-ance.

A fourth line of argument focuses attention on the obstacles to industrialization faced by most African countries. The lack of education and low levels of health and literacy already re-ferred to seriously affect the quality of skilled labour and the development of technical and managerial skills at all levels. Technical assistance and technology from advanced countries is often expensive and 'tied' in one way or another; it is also frequently inappropriate and inadvertently perpetuates the neo-colonial relationship referred to earlier. Shortage of capital, too, is endemic. With the exception of South Africa and the 'oil states', all African countries lack the domestic capital to finance adequately their own development and are obliged to borrow or receive loans and grants from the industrially advanced countries or from international agencies. The domestic market for industrial development is almost everywhere too narrow, both in terms of simple population numbers and in terms of purchasing power. And external markets are little better than they were in colonial times: it has been very difficult for African nations to build up a manufacturing industry for products for export when other African countries were doing the same, and when the established pattern of international trade between the richer and poorer countries tended to exclude penetration by African products. This whole problem is very much the concern of, among many other bodies, UNCTAD.

Another, fifth, reason sometimes put forward to help explain the low level of material development in Africa is that agriculture, which remains by far the most widespread economic activity in the continent, involving some 60–70 per cent of the work force, is consistently being given insufficient attention or investment; a sound agricultural base for subsequent industrialization and a more diversified economic structure is therefore not being laid. And it is true that although a good deal of lip-service is paid to agriculture, most African countries do little to ensure that it both is and is seen to be a priority. Public expenditure allocations on agriculture are commonly between 5 and 10 per cent of total public expenditure, and operations like the Nigerian 'Operation Feed the Nation' are symptomatic of the attitude taken by most governments towards agriculture. This kind of operation is now common in Africa; and the rationale lying behind it is obvious and laudable. Yet it can also have its dangers. For it can be interpreted as an indication that a government believes in the notion that people can grow their own food as a kind of part-time or fringe activity; it suggests that agriculture, as an industry, is not the real basis of an economy; and it implies that agriculture should not receive major priority in public investment. It is remarkable that shifting-field cultivation is still the dominant system of agricultural land-use in Africa. It has been suggested elsewhere that one of the reasons for this fact is the generally low density of population in Africa, making the change from shifting-field agriculture to permanent-field agriculture neither likely nor logical; only in those areas with 'contained' populations living at high densities (as with the Cabrais of northern Togo) does one find in Africa indigenous, pre-colonial permanent-field systems of agriculture. But however a changed attitude towards technological change and productivity in agriculture is brought about – whether by increased population densities or by the acceptance of innovations of the kind demonstrated, for instance, by the Chinese in Senegal and Sierra Leone – then the important stage of permanent-field cultivation, with all its attendant attitudinal as well as economic implications, will be a long time developing.

Many other reasons are advanced to explain economic failure or stagnation in Africa – inadequate administrative structures, irrelevant and damaging policies of too-rapid indigenization, an emphasis on such parasitical developments as the tourist industry, and many others. It is certain, for instance, that the non-oil-producing black African countries suffer very severely with an increase in oil prices from OPEC; oil accounts for a quarter of all imports by value in these black African countries. But, either taken separately or together, none of these lines of argument can really 'explain' the lack of economic progress in Africa today, except perhaps at the most general level.

It is more important to view the question and its answers within the context of a particular African state rather than from the viewpoint of Africa as a large and diverse continent. For any particular country, admittedly, the same fundamental questions must be asked. What are the aims of development? From what ideological assumptions does economic planning start? To what type of economy and society are the planners aspiring? What forces for social and economic change are already at work within the country? What kind of external assistance is likely to be offered and to be acceptable? How large a role is the whole development planning operation to play in shaping the country's future? But the answers to even such basic questions as these will differ greatly from one country to another. In the last analysis it is always the actions of a

94

particular government at a particular time that determine the direction and scope of economic policy. And if any government is to remain in power in Africa it has at least to demonstrate some ability to deal with the natural and universal ambitions of Africans for material progress – for that 'perceptible and cumulative' rise in the standards of living of an increasing proportion of the population which we earlier accepted as our working definition of development.

But why is all this relevant to the issues of African affairs with which we are concerned in these pages? The answer lies partly in the simple fact that to many Africans, at least, economic development is *the* 'affair' with which they are most clearly, closely and deeply involved. To most Africans the issues of colonialism and neo-colonialism, the question of international or regional boundaries, ethnicity, élitism, and national, regional or African unity – all are either quite irrelevant or are of only peripheral interest compared with their real day-to-day problems of earning a living, and searching for a more satisfactory way of life and wider opportunities for themselves and their families. Thus the matters of immediate concern to a Yoruba farmer engaged in the production of food crops – yams, cassava, maize and beans – for his family and for disposal in the local market place, as well as in the production of some cocoa for the local cocoa-buying agent, are his productivity, what prices he can get for his produce, better access roads, good drinking water, clinics and schools. These are the matters with which he is most deeply concerned, and to ignore this fact is to engage in little more than an irrelevant academic exercise.

The same is true of any doctrinaire or ideological analysis of African affairs. It is easy, from an African socialist standpoint, to argue that Togo or Kenya are not experiencing true economic development; that these countries' economies are as externally dependent as they were in colonial times; that both structurally and regionally these societies are becoming more rather than less unequal; and that they are becoming more rather than less class-structured. And yet if the Togolese or Kenyans perceive themselves to be becoming better off, their opportunities to be widening, and a sense of national achievement to be developing, then there is no point in saying that they are not developing, that they are being led astray and are victims of internal or external political, capitalistic propaganda; and that because one does not believe in 'the modernization process', then no such process can be occurring. Rightly or wrongly there is the feeling that development *is* taking place in both Togo and Kenya. Similarly it is no good saying that because in Tanzania élitism and corruption are being controlled, spatial and social inequalities are being evened out, and the pursuit of gross materialism eschewed, that development is taking place, if at the same time the majority of Tanzanians, especially when comparing their lot with that of Kenyans across the border – and more especially, of course, with the Kikuyu élite in Nairobi rather than with their immediate neighbours, the Masai – do not perceive themselves to be receiving what they believe to be the necessary material benefits of and opportunities for 'the good life'.

More directly, it is worth pointing out that the polarization of views between the two major 'schools' of thought about development referred to earlier – between the 'under-development-dependency' school and the 'developmentalists' – is to some extent misleading. Writers on economic matters in Africa are increasingly taking their inspiration from elsewhere – notably from writers on the political economy of Latin America – and are providing the same kind of historically based and essentially negative analyses of African economic, social and political affairs. Yet when one looks carefully at these analyses the differences between the new 'radical' and the old 'reactionary' views seem to be partly a matter of words. The other part of the difference is a matter of whether one prefers to be doctrinaire or pragmatic: whether one wishes to wrap up one's analysis and solutions in an ideological package of predictable content or whether one wishes to take each set of problems as at least to some extent unique, and work from the existing realities and latent tendencies to change within an economy or society. As Singer has pointed out,[21] no one who has even the briefest field acquaintance with Africa or made any study at all of African economic history would quarrel with many of the statements made by members of the underdevelopment-dependency school: that African governments and economies are far too dependent on the outside, rich world for aid, trade, investment, technology, and decisions of all kinds; that the power of élite groups in Africa is too great and largely self-perpetuating; that multinational companies may be harmful; that their colonial history has left most African countries with a series of often intractable problems to face; that spatial inequalities, especially between metropolitan centres and their peripheries, are too great; that the maximization of material growth should not be the chief goal of development; that most development 'models' are naïve and misleading – nothing more than heuristic devices. Conventional developmentalists believe all this as much as do conventional Marxists. But does it mean that in order to accept all these self-evident truths we must necessarily enshrine them in a particular doctrine? In the real world of today, African governments – governments which exist and have power (whether legitimate or not) to make changes and direct their economies and societies in par-ticular directions – seem desperately to need sound, practical advice about how to deal with poverty in their countries. Yet the radical argument embodies views which are essentially negative – to break up the existing colonial patterns, to break up dependency, to destroy the existing social and political system which perpetuates the present economic underdevelop-ment, and to destroy inequalities of all kinds. In other words it offers only revolutionary change with all its evils and un-certainties. The Marxist underdevelopment-dependency school deals in truisms and prejudices; it deals with poverty only by making it a factor in an intellectual exercise; and it creates an atmosphere in which economic failure becomes almost a virtue. This will provide little comfort for the mass of Africa's rural and urban poor.

This whole issue has been given some emphasis here because, as pointed out earlier in this chapter, the underdevelopment-dependency school of thought is gaining ground rapidly in many countries of Africa. It can be argued that this holds serious dangers for African governments. The problem with all ideological analyses of African affairs – especially, perhaps, economic affairs – is that they are depressingly negative and predictable, and that they tend to ignore the basic empirical experience or even the simple needs and expressed desires of the mass of the people they pretend to champion.

Development planning

All development plans in Africa nowadays are social and political as well as economic documents. And while, like all such plans, they contain a degree of rhetoric, they do give some indication of the public priorities given to various sectors of the economy and of the economic, social and political ends to which governmental economic policy is being directed. In spite of Africa's widespread poverty and low *per capita* incomes, the general statement that all its countries are, in their development plans, aiming to raise *per capita* incomes, grossly over-simplifies the issue for those countries where the decisive criteria of successful development are more social, political or even strategic rather than purely economic or material. Thus whereas in one country the overriding objective is a high rate of growth of income, in another it may be full employment, the creation of strategic industries, the reduction of reliance on foreign trade, or the furtherance of a socialist society.

Development plans in Africa are also useful documents in that they give some insight into the philosophy lying behind governmental action and policy-making. Especially in Africa, where the nation-building process still has far to go, governments hope that development plans will encourage people to participate more actively in this process, and to this extent are concerned as much with directing people's attitudes as with attaining specific economic goals. The development plan is thus seen as a means of mobilizing the energies and activities of the people, of giving the nation a common purpose and so a greater degree of cohesion. Equally, however, the attitude of a people towards any plan is a critical factor in its success or failure. An essential ingredient of successful planning is thus the encouragement of popular interest and enthusiasm and, if possible, a measure of popular participation in the whole planning process.

While national economic planning may be considered to be vital to economic progress, and so to national stability and cohesion, there is plenty of evidence in Africa that such planning must also take into account the problem of spatial inequalities and regional disparities, especially if it is to achieve its social and political ends. It has already been necessary on many occasions throughout the present chapter, as well as in earlier pages, to mention the problems of spatial inequalities of wealth in a country, and the difficulties such inequalities pose in terms of effecting national unity. At one level of analysis this problem is most clearly observed in the inequalities and disparities between urban and rural life in Africa. In Africa, as elsewhere, economic development tends to express itself far too quickly in rapid urbanization and urban growth, certainly far too quickly to avoid the major evils associated with rapid urbanization. Cities like Lagos epitomize the negative aspects of rapid urban growth – the move into the city of the younger, most useful sections of the rural population, urban unemployment, crime, the breakdown of physical and social services, appalling congestion of traffic, and the near breakdown of law and order. At the same time these larger urban centres contain the majority of the élite groups, living a lifestyle which is so far removed from that of the mass of the urban proletariat that eventual conflict seems inevitable.

At a rather larger scale, there are regional disparities within states, and the inclusion of some 'regional planning' element is now becoming more common in development planning documents, as in Ghana. And in Zaïre, the peripheral geographical distribution of wealth, economic activity and development were early identified as forming an important centrifugal force in the country. In many other countries a serious north–south problem exists: the case of the Sudan has already been instanced. Throughout the southern coastal states of West Africa, too, from Ivory Coast in the west to Nigeria in the east, the north–south problem is critical. In Ivory Coast the interdependence of some degree, at least, of regional equality and political stability is implicit in many of the planning documents. Here the sole legal party, PDCI (Parti Démocratique de Côte d'Ivoire), has argued for giving more aid for development to the poorer regions of the country 'in order to ensure continued stability of the country's affairs'.

At all levels and at all scales the essentially interdependent nature of economic and socio-political matters cannot be over-emphasized. Although it is convenient to treat the economic and political problems of Africa as distinct, the newly independent nations are rapidly being forced to become aware that to make such a distinction is arbitrary, misleading and even dangerous. In all African affairs there seem to be periods when this truism is forgotten, or at least ignored, and sudden changes of direction and policy – and even of governments – ensue. The deeply fundamental ways in which economic realities can affect not only internal but also external relations is clear from the case of Egypt. After a period of military activity, backed up by the Soviet Union, and involvement in the Middle East War with Israel, Egypt found her economy shattered. She subsequently cut off relations with Russia, and is now desperately seeking a settlement in the Middle East, so that she can concentrate on the rapidly deteriorating economic situation at home. The recent internal riots – however they are interpreted – are but one indication of the economic and social failure of Egypt's domestic policies. And Sadat is only too well aware that unless the economic base can be secured then no political success – least of all the creation of a unified, coherent nation state – can ever be achieved.

6 National unity

In discussing national unity some of the factors with which we must necessarily be concerned have already been identified. The problem of creating an effective sense of national unity or cohesion in any African country is clearly not simply a political matter: it is also part of a wider complex of economic, social, historical and psychological issues. The obstacles to unity are many and varied. Some states, like Gambia, Togo or Rwanda, might appear to be too small for viable national units, while others, like Sudan, Nigeria and Zaïre could reasonably be considered to be too large for newly independent and therefore relatively inexperienced administrations to govern. Indeed, there is something to be said for the view that small size is an important advantage, though clearly by itself it is not a sufficient condition for the creation of a sense of national unity. Togo certainly seems to be beginning to take advantage from its small size; and Tunisia, the most securely united of the

North African independent states, has a territory small and compact enough to be governed directly from Tunis without causing any marked regional antagonisms. Then many states are, so it is frequently argued, too small in population (many of them having well under 3,000,000 inhabitants) to provide the necessary human resources for a viable state in the modern world; this argument has formed the basis of many movements for regional cooperation. Again, Africa is a storehouse of awkwardly shaped states: the Caprivi Strip of Namibia, the Cabinda exclave of Angola, the bow-tie shapes of Zambia and Mali, and the narrow insertion of Gambia into Senegal. A related issue is the landlocked nature of fourteen African states and the near-landlockedness of others. African states striving for national unity have also to contend with their colonial legacies, not only in terms of the very patterns of states which have caused the problems of size and shape to which we have just referred, nor only in terms of the many boundary problems which have resulted from the European partition of the African continent, but also in terms of a host of other characteristics – of language, education, forms of settlement and the externally oriented colonial export economies. The previous chapters have also shown that ethnicity is a crucial factor in the drive for national unity in almost every African state. In many parts of Africa the ethnic group is perhaps the nearest indigenous approximation to the nation state and to this extent the conflict between ethnicity and nationalism, albeit in many varied forms, was always inevitable. National unity is also deeply affected by the existence of old and new forms of élitism, including the white élitism as expressed in South Africa's apartheid policy. And the previous chapter identified the essentially interlocking nature of economic progress and social and political development.

But these are only a few of the many possible variables affecting national unity in African countries. Perhaps the best way of drawing out the widest possible range of factors is to look first of all at a particular case-study – that of Zaïre.

National unity in Zaïre

Many circumstances have combined to produce in Zaïre a complex of tensions and polarities which impede the development of a stable, unified state. According to some writers the most important of these has been the legacy of Belgian colonial rule. The most common criticism of Belgian colonial policy is that it miscalculated the force and speed of political change in mid-twentieth-century Africa: little or no political progress was made until 1958, so that at independence in 1960 there was no nucleus of Congolese with any considerable political experience. Furthermore, Belgian administrative institutions did not appear to have great relevance for the independent state. Although the Belgians had attempted a nominal form of indirect rule, their severely centralized system of administration had tended in practice to undermine the authority of traditional chiefs, whose cooperation formed the basis of effective indirect rule in British Africa. And the suddenness with which the Belgians finally handed over power was a crucial factor in precipitating the Congo crisis of 1960.

One can argue, then, that to a great extent the Belgian colonial period made it difficult for Congo Kinshasa, as it first became on independence, to achieve effective national unity. However, the rapid handover of power from the Belgians to the Congolese was inevitable and could not reasonably have been anticipated, just as it was not anticipated by the British in their territories. Nationalist assertion developed with exceptional speed in most parts of Africa during the 1950s and pressures from anti-colonial world powers and agencies – the United States and United Nations – were reinforced by the Leopoldville (Kinshasa) riots of 1959, just before independence. And from the Belgian point of view there was the desire to protect and secure their economic investments, particularly in the Katanga region of the south-east. Furthermore, while Belgian policy made its own contribution to the forces of disintegration in the Congo, it also created some basis for unity – a common language and culture, a common currency, a good system of universal primary education and sound social and economic foundations. Thus, while it is impossible to discount altogether the centrifugal effects of Belgian colonial rule, there is some justification for the suggestion that many of the present problems of Zaïrian unity derive more from a combination of physical and cultural circumstances than from the country's historical legacy.

In the first place, Zaïre today suffers from its great size and almost completely landlocked nature. Then the very fact that much of the country is structurally a basin has, in these equatorial lowland conditions, tended to push settlement and economic life out towards the periphery – towards the higher, healthier and mineralized rim and away from the relatively inhospitable centre. The population density, moreover, is low. And the very complex pattern of ethnic groups has had a divisive effect: as far as ethnic and linguistic complexity is concerned, Nigeria is probably the only other country which can compare with Zaïre. Integration is also made difficult by the uneven pattern of economic development in the country. The two major economic core areas, around which the processes of social mobilization have been most intensive, are Kinshasa, formerly Leopoldville, in the north-west of the country, and Lubumbashi, in the south-east. These two cities occupy excentric positions. The remarkable integrated rail and river system of transport in Zaïre was something of a unifying factor: but even this system has been unable in independence to integrate effectively the widely separated and often highly discrete communities in a country the size of Zaïre.

Zaïre, then, has no physical or cultural unity, and at independence it did not even have that fragile basis for the future cooperation of disparate ethnic groups provided in Anglophone territories by a western educated élite, by African representation, and by the freedoms created by a local press and political parties. The former six provinces of the Congo expressed not only administrative convenience but also the great diversity of this vast country. Leopoldville Province, controlling the single narrow outlet to the sea, was the commercial and administrative heart. Equateur, backward and isolated, had some important European-owned plantations of rubber and oil palm. Orientale was very much less remote: from Stanleyville, that province had connections downstream to the coast as well as by road north-eastwards and eastwards to the Sudan; in Orientale, too, Africans were much more involved in cash agriculture – oil palm, rubber, cotton and coffee. Kasai Province produced diamonds and basic foodstuffs – cassava, maize and vegetables for the main towns and industrial centres of Leopoldville and Katanga. Kivu Province, on the edge of the East African plateau, possessed many of the most valuable cash-crop plantations. And finally, in the south-east, was Katanga, in many ways much more closely linked to Zambia than to the Congo, and containing the bulk of the mining and industrial activity of the country.

The divisive effects of all these circumstances, social, physical and economic, as well as the more narrowly historical factors, have continued well into independence. Zaïre remains a territorial framework with little basis for national strength or unity, and this has expressed itself in a number of secession movements, of which the most serious have been in Katanga (now Shaba). The civil war in Zaïre was provoked by the attempted secession of its richest province. The Katanga problem has never been a simple issue of ethnic feeling or separatism. Like most secession movements in Africa, the secession of Katanga in 1960 was not so much the result of the fear of domination of one group by another as the result of a convergence of a combination of historical, economic and social circumstances. To this extent Katanga epitomizes the whole Zaïrian problem today.

Although the boundary between Katanga and Zambia in the south-east of Zaïre follows for several hundred miles the divide or watershed between the Zaïre and Zambezi rivers' headstreams, this watershed is hardly perceptible on the ground. In its topography, as in its geology and mineral resources, Katanga is part of the Central African copperbelt. The economic history of Katanga is certainly most closely tied to that of its southern neighbour and it was from the south, and not from the north, that the railway first penetrated into the Katanga mining area. Climatically, Katanga is well suited to European occupation and at independence about half the Belgians in Zaïre lived along the railway line from the Zambian border to Bukama in Katanga. The settler population in Katanga had close affinities with settlers in Zambia and Rhodesia, and this made the idea of secession economically and politically attractive to Europeans. As for the Africans, many of the African labourers in the Katanga mining and industrial area came originally not from Katanga but from the heavily populated trusteeship and now independent territories of Rwanda and Burundi over 1,000 miles to the north. The arguments for secession were very powerful indeed and geographical realities made and continue to make the movement for Katanga secession entirely logical. But from the point of view of Zaïre the secession of Katanga could have only disastrous effects. For without Katanga Zaïre loses much of its justification as a viable political and economic unit. Katanga provides a great deal of the country's wealth – estimates vary from 45 per cent to 80 per cent. On the other hand it is to be questioned whether Zaïre can afford to endure for long what has been called 'Katanganization' – the acceptance by Zaïrians of the argument that the vast economic resources of Katanga must necessarily entitle its leaders to a dominant position in the government of the country.

The case of Katanga is the most obvious and significant case of secessionism in Zaïre. Another example is Kasai, though this is much more clearly an expression of true ethnic feelings. In Kasai, with its diamond and gold mining, the secession issue arises from a complex north–south problem which is emphasized by the location of the two provincial capitals of Luluabourg and Bakwaya lying close together on the main railway. At independence the Luba people were driven south by the Lulua majority and, as a result, the population of southern Kasai rose from 300,000 in 1958 to 1,300,000 in 1963, the population of Bakwaya itself increasing from 40,000 to 200,000 in the same period. The leader of the Luba, one Kalonji, rallied the Luba into his breakaway state – 'Kalonji's Diamond Republic' – but such was the rate of immigration of refugees from the north that the new 'state' was soon overwhelmed, food production and distribution proved impossible, many died from starvation, labour problems intensified, and the movement collapsed.

Another secessionist problem in Zaïre is that of Bakongo. This again is primarily ethnic in origin but is greatly exacerbated here by the fact that the boundaries between Zaïre, Angola and the former French Congo cut through the lands of the Bakongo, who are today distributed between three independent nation states. Yet other examples of incipient secessionism lie in the north-east near the border with Sudan, and in the extreme east, in Kivu country. Here Gizenga's Soviet-backed 'Democratic Forces for the Liberation of the Congo' have been operating for some time and an armed struggle is developing between these forces and the central government forces of Mobutu. According to Gizenga the civil servants and military in the east are not being paid, the roads are not maintained and there is social and economic chaos. Certainly there is chronic instability in Zaïre's eastern province, and many reports suggest that the picture is not dissimilar elsewhere in the country.

The problems of achieving unity in Zaïre are clearly formidable, though probably no more formidable than in many other African states. According to some Zaïrians it demands the creation of some form of federal constitution which would allow the greatest degree of regional autonomy within the framework of a nation state covering the whole of Zaïre. But other Zaïrians believe that a strongly centralized or unitarian approach is necessary. This is a long-standing difference of opinion. At independence in 1960 those arguing for centralized control had 71 seats, while the federalists had 66 – a very evenly balanced situation. But the largest single party was Lumumba's MNC (unitarian party) which therefore came to form the government in the critical opening months of independence. But since then, and in particular since the assassination of Lumumba, federalism has gained ground, though the clash between unitarians and federalists continues to lie at the very heart of Zaïrian politics, as one would expect in a country of such great size and diversity. Partly with the aim of reducing the power of large regional interests in Zaïre, the former 6

provinces of the Belgian Congo were divided, in 1963, into 21
administrative units, Katanga alone being divided into 3 units.
With the federal territory of Kinshasa, this gave a total of 22
divisions. But this re-drawing of internal provincial boundaries
was subsequently criticized as indicating a reversal to 'tribalism'
– the Bakongo, for instance, now had their own province in
Zaïre – though in fact only 6 of the 21 provinces could in any
way be recognized as ethnic entities; indeed several other
considerations, including distance from a provincial capital,
had been taken into account in re-drawing the provincial
boundaries. The 22 administrative divisions were later found
to be too unwieldy, however, and were re-grouped into 11
and subsequently into 19 provinces. Here is a good example –
Nigeria is another – of a state manipulating the internal administrative divisions, regions or provinces of a country in an
attempt to create a sense of national unity. But it is difficult to
see the logic of such a policy: no matter what number of states
is created some groups will still consider themselves minorities
and clamour for separate states of their own.

Apart from the need to achieve political stability and a sense
of national unity, one urgent requirement in Zaïre, as in so
many African states, is physical security. The need for peace
and security in Zaïre was accentuated by the civil war, by
rebellions and by the activities of the United Nations in the
country after independence. As Perham has put it, 'the story
of the Congo's independence is, in its own context, as blood-
stained and involved as that of its creation under King Leopold II'.[22] The economic effects of the disorders within Zaïre
were initially disastrous, most agricultural and industrial
production being affected. In 1965 production was still only
80 per cent of what it was at independence: five years of independence had reduced the wealth of the country by one-fifth,
living standards had deteriorated, and the essential independence of political progress and social and economic prosperity had been more than adequately demonstrated. Fully
restored and given access to expanding world markets, the
agricultural areas of Zaïre have great potential – a number of
them export products, especially animal and vegetable oils,

cotton, coffee, tea, spices and fruits. Petroleum is now being produced near the Zaïre estuary, and there is still a great potential for diamond mining in Kasai and for copper and other mining in Katanga. The hydro-electric resources of the Congo river are almost certainly the greatest of any country in the world. A rapid programme of industrialization has been started and a large steel mill near Kinshasa constructed. Given peace and security the economic potential of Zaïre is impressive.

The immediate omens, however, are far from favourable. The Zaïrian government has recently (1976) been reorganized in the Mouvement Populaire de la Révolution (MPR) and this was needed

> because the country was beginning the second decade of its revolution in a very difficult period; in the economic field its situation was unfavourable; and its means of egress were blocked by the troubled situation in Angola and its transport networks being unusable and the flagrant aggression of the joint Russian–Cuban forces.[23]

Zaïre's national unity, like that of so many other countries, may not in the end be entirely in her own hands. She certainly has a tremendous debt burden and dependency on the west, especially the United States, which must to some extent explain the United States' interest in maintaining Zaïre's territorial integrity.

Secession and irredentist movements

So many of the points made about Zaïre and the problems it faces in striving for national unity have their counterpart elsewhere in the continent, and the centrifugal forces at work within states are perhaps most clearly demonstrated in the numerous secession movements in Africa. Just as, so it was argued in an earlier chapter, boundary problems seem likely to increase in number and severity, so secession movements seem likely also to become a more common problem in contemporary African affairs. Whether the term 'secession' is used here correctly is a matter of opinion. Some of the so-called secession movements identified in Zaïre in the preceding section are perhaps more accurately simply regional rebellions against the central government in which a reorganization of power-sharing is only one factor. But at least it is important to recognize and accept the distinction between 'secessionism', which originates from within a state, and 'irredentism', where the stimulus for change comes from outside.

Perhaps the best-known secession movement in Africa since independence has been that of Biafra, in Nigeria, on which a great deal has already been written. The most recent significant potential secession movements, however, include not only those already identified in Zaïre – Katanga, Bakongo, Kivu and Kasai – but also those in southern Sudan, in Ethiopia (Eritrea) and in northern Chad. As for irredentist movements, one example takes us back to the Ewe where, in south-eastern Ghana, some of the Ewe have reacted strongly to the recent reorganization in Ghana which, by reducing the Ewe representation in government, is regarded as having ended the ethnic neutrality of the Ghanaian military regime. The clandestine NLMWT (National Liberation Movement of Western Togoland), said to be active on both sides of the border, is now campaigning to rejoin neighbouring Togo. Other important examples of increasing significance are in the areas of Ogaden (Ethiopia) and north-eastern Kenya, where the stimulus to change comes from their Somali kinsmen in Somalia.

These examples give some indication of the many causes of secession or irredentism. Geographical considerations include large size and awkward shape, lack of territorial contiguity, striking ecological contrasts, and peripheral or excentric locations of populations and centres of economic activity, as well as the arbitrariness of national boundaries. Ethnicity and other cultural differences – especially in language and religion – are also significant, as are differences in commercial attitudes and political aims and ideologies among rival groups or parties within states. In some cases, too, irredentism seems to arise partly from the clash of personalities and competing social or élite groups. And it is only too clear in some cases – as in Katanga – that secessionism, as well as irredentism, may have its origins in the interests of external forces such as neighbouring countries, the former metropolitan countries, or one or other of the major world powers. Yet while it is possible to list in this way so many causes of secession movements in Africa, each one represents a unique mix of many of these causes, the emphasis varying from case to case. It is also important to note that in Africa there are examples of territorial secession which are deliberately created by national governments, the most obvious case being the Bantustan policy of the South African government in which quite separate nations, like Transkei, are being created.

The main attraction of secession is that it makes more likely a better future and the achievement of a sense of national identity and unity in the territory wishing to secede; furthermore, it removes from the parent nation a serious threat to its own nationhood. It is also an important argument that secession may simply express a natural realignment of national territorial boundaries which were arbitrarily and frequently illogically drawn by the former colonial powers in Africa. The main argument against secession, however, is that successful secession would certainly breed more secession and result in innumerable and endless inter-state conflicts, instabilities and many more new states in Africa. As we have already seen, the OAU has ruled against boundary changes and so, quite specifically, against secession movements.

Nevertheless, all the present evidence suggests that secession movements are likely to increase in number and intensity in Africa over the next decade or so. And whether governments will be able to control these movements and reduce the stresses they will undoubtedly produce will provide African leaders with one of their greatest challenges.

Regions, internal states and capitals

Reference has already been made, in this and in earlier chapters, to the fact that attempts have been made in many African states to achieve a more effective and unified state structure by dividing the country into several regions with some degree of autonomy (as in Kenya) or into several internal states (as in Nigeria). While size, incipient irredentism, ethnicity or any other factor might determine the need for such a structure, there seems to be no evidence that it is ever likely to lead to the creation of a strong sense of national cohesion and therefore of national purpose. Multi-state structures, especially, are very expensive – they encourage bureaucracy, centralization and inefficiency, rather than efficiency and decentralization. Regional and state divisions within a country, where, as in Africa, nationalism is not yet a strong, positive force on which a government can rely, preclude the very end for which they are set up. They are not only irrelevant: they are likely to be positively damaging to the cause of national unity. Inter-regional and inter-state rivalries are already common features of the African social, economic and political scene.

Some writers also question any attempt to try to foster a sense of national unity by shifting the national capital to some more 'central' or 'non-controversial' part of a country. In Tanzania, the logic of shifting the capital from Dar es Salaam to Dodoma in attempts to reduce regional inequalities and to remove the concentration of wealth, economic activity and élite-style living from the coastal capital is obvious. The political motivation is clearly overriding and, in the case of Nigeria, the plan to move the capital from Lagos to the Abuja area of central Nigeria is explicitly 'to bring government nearer the people and ensure future political stability'. Abuja has a central geographical position in Nigeria, it has a reasonably good climate and good water resources, and the area is not clearly associated with any one ethnic group. The commercial capital will remain at Lagos. It is, however, difficult to see how Abuja will bring government 'nearer the people' when one of the outstanding attributes of the Abuja site is that it is located in an area of very low population density.

In other cases, however, the shifting of the capital has been a necessary expedient. One example is in Mauritania, where it was decided as early as the late 1950s to undertake the construction of a new capital at Nouakchott to supersede the old capital, St Louis, which was not even in Mauritania but across the river in Senegal. Located at a relatively cool and breezy point midway along the coast between the desert north and the more humid south, and not firmly in any one ethnic area, Nouakchott symbolizes the attempt to build a viable Mauritanian state. Another case is Gaberone, built by the British for Botswana, which was previously ruled from Mafeking.

Nationalism and types of government

Historically, African nationalism has always been essentially negative or anti-colonial and could never be expressed as a desire to win back freedom and independence by former nation states. In large measure it had been left to the European colonial powers to create the basis or framework for true nationalism, even at the level of the ethnic group. Although a number of writers use the terms 'nation', 'state' and 'country', interchangeably, it is important to emphasize that a true nation, in the sense of one with a common culture, language and historical experience, is most closely approximated in Africa by the ethnic group. Somalia is perhaps Africa's only true nation state. Otherwise, nations as such are rarely indigenous to Africa – possible exceptions are Somalia, Botswana and Transkei – and have mostly been constructed in the post-independence period. The need to develop true nationality – a 'nation myth' or 'state idea' – is indeed one of the most intractable problems in Africa today.

The difficulties of achieving this are to some extent common to all countries in Africa, but each state also has its own special problems. Nigeria's special difficulties arise from her great size and diversity, which until 1966 was expressed politically through ethnically dominated regional governments – the Yoruba in the west, the Ibo in the east and the Hausa in the north. Only in the Mid-West Region was there no single dominant ethnic group, although this fourth region was formed largely as a result of dissatisfaction by the Edo-speaking

113

groups with the Yoruba-dominated Western Region of which the Mid-West was formerly a part. Today, with nineteen 'states' and an avowedly anti-ethnic military regime, it remains to be seen whether a sense of nationhood can be imposed upon the undercurrents of ethnic antagonisms which remain so characteristic of this vast and most populous of African countries.

As for the different types of government in Africa today, the multi-party administrations bequeathed to most African countries by the former colonial powers have for the most part disappeared, though there are still examples of multi-party governments and of governments which are moving back to this system: Senegal, for instance, has recently decided to permit three parties in the country; and in Egypt the multi-party system is still regarded as synonymous with democracy, three legal parties being allowed to operate. There are also a few of what in modern Africa appear strangely anachronistic monarchies; indeed one, in the Central African Republic – now the Empire of Central Africa – was set up as late as 1976. The monarchy in Morocco (King Hassan) seems to be entrenched, in spite of several abortive attempts at coups of one form or another; that of February 1977 was led by left-wing rebels in an attempt to overthrow the government and establish a 'People's Republic' in Morocco.

But in general, African governments are now one-party or military governments of some kind. Many western observers regard the trend towards the one-party state as undesirable, implying as it does a revolt against the Westminster model of parliamentary democracy and carrying with it the seeds of totalitarian dictatorships. It is argued that opposition to one-party states can only be expressed through violence – hence the large number of coups and military regimes in the continent. But on the other hand it is not impossible for a one-party state to provide not only for a peaceful change of government but also for democracy. In the Sudan's one-party system, national and regional assembly members are drawn not only from territorial constituencies, but also from broad-based interest groups such as intellectuals and the trade unions.

And in Tanzania, provisions to ensure this are written into the constitution and at elections the electorate, while voting for one party, choose between contesting candidates, who may lie along a broad ideological spectrum. In such a situation free and complete debate may be allowed within the party, and opposition allowed as long as a member is not in the cabinet. It is possible to ensure that every policy which is being opposed by or causing concern to the public is brought into parliament and discussed. Furthermore, it is frequently argued that a one-party state in Africa is appropriate, in that African society often lacks those rigid class divisions upon which competing political parties in developed countries have so often been based; a multi-party system in Africa tends to crystallize along ethnic lines. Again, as one Ghanaian paper has put it, 'party politics is too colonial, an alien system, and kicks against Africa's natural social organization. That is why it has been rejected by almost all independent African states.'[24] It could also be pointed out that one of the main reasons for the rigidities of the South African and Rhodesian governments is precisely because both operate a multi-party system. However authoritarian the present South African government may appear, it operates within a multi-party democracy for the whites; it must be responsive to its own electorate and this imposes a major constraint on it in any attempt to change its racial policies. In Rhodesia the present attempt by Ian Smith to abolish racial discrimination, referred to in an earlier chapter, has run into serious opposition from the right wing of the ruling Rhodesian Front party which Smith leads. Both Vorster and Smith, indeed, are prisoners of the multi-party democratic system.

Certainly it is true that most of the one-party governments in Africa have been created with the overriding aim of achieving effective national unity. Kaunda's purpose in creating his one-party government in Zambia in 1972 was quite explicitly to reinforce the sense of national unity in the country. In Zambia, as always when a multi-party system has been inherited by Africans from colonial rulers, policies had been bedevilled up to 1972 by ethnic conflicts. Without a class structure the various parties had inevitably polarized around ethnic groups. At the same time, because Zambia is landlocked and surrounded by a number of hostile countries, her rival parties offered constant opportunities for foreign subversion. The multi-party system in Zambia was proving inimical to both nation-building and to economic development. The one-party system, it was hoped, would enable all Zambians to concentrate on the paramount task of social and economic development.

As for military governments, these have not invariably resulted from the existence of a one-party state, having occurred also in Nigeria. And it would be absurd to suggest that all, or even most, of the military governments in Africa are or have been especially repressive. The military rule in Togo, for instance, is clearly fair and effective and has acquired a degree of legitimacy in the country which few governments in multi-party states could match. In some states, such as the Sudan under Nimeiri, what began as a military government has increasingly become government by meritocracy, with the army being used as the instrument for a change of government rather than simply to impose military rule. If one examines the performance of military regimes in Africa, indeed, it is impossible not to conclude, with McKinley and Cohan, that they are not universally different from non-military-regime systems of government.[25] Systems which have experienced military regimes are not restricted to the weaker economic systems – Nigeria is the outstanding case in point. Their economic performances, too, compare favourably with non-military regime systems and, despite military rule, they do not in general have larger armed forces or greater military expenditure than non-military governments.

It is true that military governments may have lower levels of political activity and so more political instability; but they do not have more economic instability. The problem with military governments is primarily one of how to transfer control from military to civilian rule. This is a problem which Nigeria, having experienced a series of military governments since January 1966, may have to face by the end of 1978. The same is true of Ghana where, writing of the military governor's plans to hand over to civilian rule by 1979, one newspaper commentator has noted:

> Ghanaians have been here before. No political change could have been more carefully organized and thoughtfully planned than the return to civilian rule in 1969. But within three years the army was back. Nobody regrets the civilian rule period ending. Opposition to the present government is more likely to come from within than outside – one of the inherent weaknesses of military rule.[26]

The Ghana case is indeed an interesting one. As the first black African country to become independent in 1957, with a relatively educated and integrated society, and with what was then one of the highest levels of economic development in Africa, Ghana seemed to have a secure future as one of the continent's élite states. The power and prestige of Nkrumah was unquestioned and he was perhaps the first of the great charismatic leaders of independent black Africa. Why Nkrumah was overthrown by a military coup is a matter for discussion, but certainly a series of economic failures must have had much to do with it. And although the country has now attained some small degree of economic stability, Ghana has clearly lost her prestigious position on the African continent.

The whole question of the charismatic leader is of great importance in Africa, and it would be misleading to discuss the affairs of, say, Tanzania, Senegal, Kenya, Uganda or Zambia without mentioning the powerful positions and roles played in these countries by their leaders – Nyerere, Senghor, Kenyatta, Amin and Kaunda. These men provide perhaps the main thrust and direction of policy, and in their own ways provide the integrating force for national aspirations. Some would argue that African ethnicity demands the existence of a strong, personal leadership and that no sense of national unity is likely to develop without it. The problem, of course, is that it is open to abuse and that corruption, oppression and even megalomania can destroy the very foundations of life and dignity. More importantly, perhaps, the 'personality cult' carries with it the seeds of its own destruction in the

117

disruption that is to be expected on the death or removal from office of the national leader.

Whatever type of government is to be found in African countries today, the one overriding need is certainly for a strong firm government which has legitimacy in the sense that it is supported by the majority of people. The scale at which the political factor and legitimacy operate is particularly significant in Africa where the contact between local, regional and national structures may be but slight. Certainly the authority of the local village, village-group, clan or ethnic group may well be far more effective and significant than the national or even regional government. Indeed, the issue of legitimacy of a government is probably more critical in Africa than in developed countries; as Leys argues, in Africa it is generally true that a government – for instance its policies, parliament and agricultural officers – has no generally accepted right to do the things it does in formulating policies.[27] And the most persistent and dangerous challenge to this legitimacy comes from 'the bonds of kinship, language and locality which far outweigh the "civil ties" which govern the citizen's relationship with other citizens generally and with the "civil authorities" '.

Whether this legitimacy is brought about through conventional democratic procedures, by the fortunate existence of a charismatic leader, by the one-party state or by a military government is not yet perhaps so important as the fact that a strong and firm government must somehow be created. In Africa, as in most developing countries where power has passed over to heterogeneous groups in a very short time through elections arranged by departing colonial authorities, unless there is a backbone which everybody recognizes as stiffening and controlling the nation it is futile to talk about social and economic development. On this basis the existence of a military governorship in Nigeria, with an army of some 250,000 (as compared with 15,000 before the Biafran war) is justified. Or as John Stuart Mill put it long ago, 'the early difficulties in the way of spontaneous progress are so great that there is seldom any choice of means for overcoming them; and a ruler full of the spirit of improvement is warranted in the use of any expedients that will attain an end perhaps otherwise unattainable'.[28]

Putting it another way, the real problem African governments face today is one of order, discipline and authority; they have to inculcate a sense of responsibility on the part of individuals and groups, as well as more mature and less selfish and irresponsible attitudes to relationships beyond those determined by traditional roles. Furthermore, African governments have to find ways of controlling, both in the nation and in the government, the two major motivating forces of both individuals and groups – the search for power and the search for wealth. It seems likely that none of these ends will ever be achieved except through firm government which, for some time to come, may have to forgo the luxury of conventional democratic institutions and processes.

National unity in independent African countries is clearly far from easy to achieve, but perhaps it is not surprising that this should be so, seeing that most of these states have had well under a generation in which to foster any true sense of national unity or cohesion. It is also pertinent to ask whether in any case the pursuit of national unity is necessarily desirable. An implicit assumption in almost all discussion today is that the need for such unity is axiomatic. Yet it could be argued that to create national unity and so, by implication, to encourage nationalism is the surest way both to hinder regional cooperation between states and to frustrate the ultimate goal of African unity. And it is to these last points – to the question of regional cooperation and African unity – that we now turn.

7 Regional cooperation and African unity

Regional cooperation

Many of the arguments for regional cooperation or groupings of states reflect the problems of achieving national unity referred to in the previous chapter: the small populations, awkward shapes, landlocked positions, and the apparent lack of economic, social or political viability exhibited by many states. National parochialism is fostered by the different colonial associations – by, for instance, different European languages and educational systems – and by the existing transport and communication networks. It is still difficult in Africa to move by road or rail from one state to another, and it is still easier, for instance, to telephone from Lomé (Togo) to Paris than to Accra, in Ghana, just a few miles across the border to the west. Moreover, inter-state cooperation seems vitally necessary, for instance in river basin development, and there is little doubt that groups of African states are likely to carry much more weight in international affairs than if they act singly.

However, it is no exaggeration to say that while there have been many attempts at regional cooperation in Africa, not one has yet achieved any real measure of success. It is fashionable to explain this failure by suggesting that regional cooperation in Africa must inevitably founder on the rock of nationalism. But the problem is far more complex than this and can perhaps best be illustrated by looking very briefly at a few examples.

West Africa

There would seem to be strong and compelling reasons for some sort of economic, if not political, cooperation between the fifteen states of West Africa. In no other part of the world, except perhaps Central America, is there such a large number of very small states, many of which have broadly similar economies and little economic basis for independent political existence. Furthermore, three of these states – Niger, Mali and Upper Volta – are landlocked, and so have to trade through and use port facilities in one or more of their neighbours.

Another reason for encouraging some form of cooperation between states in West Africa is to facilitate inter-state trade beyond that demonstrated by the needs of the landlocked states. It has been argued by some writers that economic cooperation of this kind in West Africa is undesirable where it implies the establishing of customs unions; for the simultaneous existence in West Africa of several dovetailing and superimposed customs unions could well lead to serious technical complications, and the economic value of a customs union which embraces isolated countries remote from their centres of gravity is thought to be questionable. Yet inter-state trade could be an important means of widening the domestic market because, with the possible exception of Nigeria, all West African states suffer from the fact that their domestic markets for their own products are inadequate.

It is true that this question of widening the domestic market in West Africa is not solely a matter of reducing the economic barriers set up by the present patchwork of political units: it is also related to the improvement and extension of transport facilities and to an increase in the purchasing power of the local population. Nevertheless, there is little doubt that the present pattern of international boundaries still works against the expansion of local markets, encourages the building of high tariff walls and, in general, helps to perpetuate the divisive tendencies in West African economic life.

Other factors suggesting the need for cooperation between West African states can receive only the briefest mention here. Some remarks have already been made about the need to reduce tariff barriers and about the opportunities for cooperation presented by the existence of ethnic communities spreading across two or more adjacent political units. In economic development, cooperation is required to facilitate large-scale planning, to avoid unnecessary duplication in research, and to solve the practical problems of developing the major West African rivers, particularly the Niger, for hydro-electric power, irrigation and navigation. Politically, too, cooperation is necessary to increase West Africa's potential for effective defence and to increase the economic and political bargaining power of the region in continental and world affairs.

On the other hand, the difficulties lying in the way of achieving any kind of regional cooperation, either in economic or political matters, are many and formidable. The fundamental dichotomy between north and south, in terms of environment, population, religion and economy; the complicated pattern of ethnic groups and languages; the different colonial associations, reflected in official languages, educational and legal systems, and in administrative frameworks; the numerous currencies and trading relations; the contrasted levels of wealth and development; and the poor communications between neighbouring states: all these factors combine to hinder cooperation at any level. Then there are the extreme inequalities in size and population among the states of West Africa, which result in the smaller nations fearing domination by the larger. Indeed, there appears to exist no widespread or deep-seated desire for regional cooperation. The concept of West Africa as a distinctive region is at best vague; and the exact form of any federation, confederation or customs union is no more agreed upon than is the method by which it might be achieved.

However, a number of attempts to form regional groupings have taken place within West Africa since the late 1950s. One of the more important of these was the Benin–Sahel Entente, established in 1959, involving loose links between Ivory Coast, Upper Volta, Niger, Benin and, later, Togo. A solidarity fund for mutual assistance into which each state paid 10 per cent of its revenue was set up; and from this Niger, Dahomey and Upper Volta each received five-sixteenths annually, while Ivory Coast received only one-sixteenth. There was close coordination of development plans, taxation policies, public administration, labour legislation, public works, transport and communications. The entente was aimed primarily at economic cooperation between the member states, although it had some political significance as an experiment in parallelism: a counter-weight to the richer Ghana that it surrounded and to Nigeria that it adjoined in the east.

The economic basis for the entente was sound. As a group of contiguous states it comprised a market of over 12,000,000 people. Its member countries had comparable administrative experience under the French, their constitutions are similar and they have the same official language and currency. For a long time there has been considerable movement of peoples and goods between these states – labourers from Upper Volta working on the coffee and cocoa farms of the Ivory Coast, and Niger labourers working in Benin – and the Ivory Coast railway and port of Abidjan are vital to the overseas trade of Upper Volta, as it is now also to that of Niger. The economic basis of the entente, too, is well diversified, ranging from the coffee, cocoa, bananas, timber and diamonds of Ivory Coast – easily the most prosperous French-speaking state in West Africa – to the oil palm of Benin, and the groundnuts and cattle products of Upper Volta and Niger.

The Benin–Sahel Entente, however, met a number of difficulties, but the most important is one which has resulted in the failure, or at least the limited success, of similar attempts in Africa over the past two decades: the great differences in wealth and levels of development of the member states. Thus the Ivory Coast, while contributing so much more than any of the other members, received relatively little and quite understandably resented what amounted to subsidizing her poorer neighbours. This is not a new development. In the 1950s the Ivory Coast had been most anxious for independence and had opposed federalism between the French-speaking states for essentially the same reason. The Ivory Coast was then providing some 40 per cent of the annual exports and nearly 90 per cent of the dollar earnings of French West Africa, but federal taxes levied from Dakar resulted in price increases of up to one-half in the Ivory Coast.

Among the French-speaking states of West Africa perhaps the greatest force for regional cooperation has been the adherence of most of these states to the concept of the French Community. In 1958 all the former French states were given the option of autonomy within the French Community or complete independence. Only Guinea opted for the latter, and joined with Ghana in the Ghana–Guinea Union. The French Community, however, soon changed radically in character and this led to other attempts at cooperation, as with the abortive Mali Federation between Senegal and Mali (then called Soudan), which broke up in 1960. The Union of African States (UAS), established in 1961 and lasting until 1964, was a later development of the Ghana–Guinea Union but also included Mali. Regarded by its member states as a nucleus for a future United States of Africa, it was open to any other state or federation accepting its aims: the pooling of resources, the liquidation of all forms of colonialism, a common planning directive, the harmonizing of foreign policies, a joint defence policy, and the rehabilitation of African culture. This UAS was an interesting experiment in that it had to grapple with a number of important problems – partial non-contiguity of the member states, two official languages, three different currencies, varying relations with former colonial rulers, poor communications between states, and widely differing levels of development. On the other hand, the UAS embraced a market of over 14,000,000 people and possessed largely non-competitive exports: Ghana's cocoa, manganese, gold, diamonds and timber; Mali's groundnuts, cotton, rice, cattle and river fish; and Guinea's coffee, bananas, iron, bauxite, alumina and diamonds. While economic cooperation between the three states was less than had been hoped for, politically it was of major importance as a first attempt to bridge the gap between the French- and English-speaking territories of West Africa.

Another example of attempted economic integration in West Africa is the (French) West African Monetary Union. This currently involves Ivory Coast, Togo, Benin, Upper Volta, Niger and Senegal. Its currency is the CFA (Communauté financière africaine) franc which is freely convertible into French francs. Several other examples of economic integration discussed in recent years include the West African Free Trade Area, to cover Sierra Leone, Guinea, Liberia and Ivory Coast, and the attempt to bring about some form of association between Senegal and Gambia, sometimes referred to as Senegambia. But by far the most important and promising attempt at regional cooperation in West Africa is the Economic Community of West African States (ECOWAS). At its first plenary session at Lomé (Togo) in November 1976 it was agreed to establish the community with all fifteen West African states as members, and it is by far the most ambitious regional grouping yet attempted in Africa.

Northern Equatorial Africa

One of the outstanding characteristics of Equatorial Africa north of Zaïre is the strength of ethnic allegiances. This is, of course, a common feature of most African countries, but perhaps nowhere in the continent are politics so clearly based on ethnic groups as they are in the northern countries of this area. Ethnic reactions to political events are the rule and a number of serious clashes between ethnic groups have taken place since independence. The independent states of former French Equatorial Africa (Chad, Central African Empire, Gabon and Congo) and Cameroon provide good support for the view that territories without a well-defined nationalist move-

125

ment are particularly susceptible to ethnic divisions; and that in the absence of an established élite and any widespread nationalist sentiment, political organization inevitably comes to depend on ethnic allegiances.

The reason for the political importance of ethnicity in these territories is not so much the actual fragmentation of ethnic communities – which is, after all, common to most of Africa – as the generally very low level of economic development, and the lack of contact between the various parts of the region. This is one of the most backward areas of Africa, characterized by great poverty, illiteracy, very low population densities, little urbanization, and a serious lack of communications both within and between the constituent states. Furthermore, there were in northern Equatorial Africa only weak foundations for the growth of political movements – no substantial trade union movement and no considerable educated community or élite. Politics in the various states remain largely attached to local feelings based on ethnic and, to some extent, on religious foundations.

On the other hand, while ethnicity has for long been a difficult problem in the area, these states did have considerable experience of politics before independence, even though it was local rather than national. While the former Belgian Congo may be said to have suffered from lack of political experience, the former states of northern Equatorial Africa may be said to have suffered from a surfeit of it.

The other important point to emphasize about these territories is that they became independent without there being any strong indigenous pressure for self-government. French Equatorial Africa is a clear example of an area that became independent as a result of external pressures rather than by its own intent. Even as late as 1956, most of the African leaders in the area would have preferred to retain strong links with France rather than take the path immediately to complete independence. Each of the four territories of French Equatorial Africa was to a greater or lesser degree aware of its economic weakness and anxious to retain French economic, technical and military support.

To strengthen their economies and to counter further balkanization, several economic and political links have been proposed between the states of northern Equatorial Africa. One of the difficulties of association has been the opposition of Gabon, as the richest of the states, in rather the same way as the Ivory Coast reacted in West Africa. Another has been the centrifugal forces represented in the Congo by the powerful Bakongo people looking across the Zaïre river to their kinsmen in Zaïre and in Angola, and in Gabon by the Fang looking northwards to the Fang in Equatorial Guinea and Cameroon. Some agreement, especially on customs matters, has, however, proved possible, partly because Gabon still needs to export its manganese through Congo, and because Chad can threaten its southern neighbours by proposing to use Nigerian rail and port facilities. A customs union between the four former countries of French Equatorial Africa – the Equatorial Customs Union (UDE) – was set up in 1959, and this was joined by Cameroon in 1961. A more recent and not wholly unsuccessful development was the setting-up of the Economic Customs Union of Central and Equatorial Africa (UDEAC). This came into operation in 1966 and is designed to facilitate a variety of connecting links between its member states, which comprise the former territories of French Equatorial Africa and Cameroon. The aim is to strengthen inter-state solidarity in economic and political matters, and it is based on the belief that the best way to achieve African cooperation and unity is through regional economic groupings.

The aims of UDEAC include the provision of communications to the sea for the landlocked states of Equatorial Africa. According to one proposal, railways will link Chad and the Central African Empire with the port and growing industrial centre of Douala in Cameroon. There are, however, two major problems associated with UDEAC. The first is the continued reluctance of Gabon to remain a member of a union from which it will apparently gain little, while being expected to contribute a great deal. To some extent this also now applies to Cameroon and the Congo, which have direct access to the coast and are more industrialized than either Chad or the Central African

Empire. The second problem relates to the location of economic, and especially industrial, projects. The cotton textile industry is a case in point. Most of the cotton is produced in Chad, Cameroon and the Central African Empire; yet there are plans to build textile mills not only in Chad and the Central African Empire but also in the Congo and in Gabon, although neither of these two latter countries grows any cotton.

Other movements for regional cooperation

To list all the movements for regional cooperation over the last decade and a half would be both tedious and pointless. One classic case of an attempt at regional cooperation that failed was the Central African Federation, set up in 1954 between what were then Northern Rhodesia, Southern Rhodesia and Nyasaland. There is no consensus of opinion about why this failed and was abandoned in 1964, but one reason may well have been that it tried to achieve political as well as economic union. One of the more important current movements, however, is the Afro-Mauritius Joint Organization (OCAM) between Benin, Gabon, Ivory Coast, Togo, Senegal, Upper Volta, Niger, Central African Empire, Rwanda and Mauritius; the Seychelles is to join after independence. This regional grouping is interesting in that it involves non-contiguous countries, from different parts of the political spectrum, and includes the smaller islands of the Indian Ocean (Mauritius and Seychelles). Another attempt at regional cooperation is the Mano River Union, between Sierra Leone and Liberia; this is a customs union between the two countries and seeks cooperation in telecommunications, silvicultural and forest projects, maritime, postal, management and agricultural training.

A further regional movement embodies the Gambia–Senegal issue raised earlier in these pages, and it is worth noting that the concept of Senegambia is not mentioned at all in the most recent agreement. Instead the two countries are trying to develop *ad hoc* arrangements of mutual benefit, notably the setting up of a River Gambia Basin Authority, the building of a bridge over the Gambia river and a road between Banjul and Kaolak. Two dams are also to be built along the Gambia river, and one, at Kakreti, will regulate the river's flow (for agricultural development); the other, at Sambangalon, will provide for electricity needed by Senegal to exploit its iron deposits further east. Again, a good example of cooperation (or, as some observers would put it, a good example of countries sharing the spoils of annexation) is the recent agreement by Morocco and Mauritania to share the lucrative phosphate mines at Bou Craa, which lie not on the agreed border between the states fixed after the withdrawal of the Spanish from the western Sahara, but well within what is now Moroccan territory.

But perhaps the best-known example in Africa of regional cooperation, largely because of its longer history, is in East Africa. The East African Community, as it is called today, was one of the first and most promising movements for regional cooperation in Africa in the period immediately following independence. Cooperation had been initiated by the East African High Commission in the East African Common Services Organization (EACSO) which provided for cooperative control of monetary, postal, transport and communications (especially railways and harbours, airways and telecommunications), medical and agricultural services and research throughout the three territories. And it was hoped that EACSO would be strengthened on independence and even extend to political unity and embrace, perhaps, such peripheral countries as Rwanda, Burundi, Malawi and Mauritius. The East African presidents committed themselves to work towards an East African federation by gradually increasing the power and functions of the community until federation was achieved.

As it has turned out, however, the East African Community has tended to wither away, and the reasons for this failure emphasize once again the apparently inevitable and irreconcilable conflicts between regional and national interests. As *The Times* put it,

disputes have punctuated the workings of the community and, since its structure relies on the authority of the three

129

presidents meeting together, its decline has accelerated because no meeting has taken place since 1971. Consequently every dispute or administrative difficulty which has occurred within the past seven or eight years has remained unresolved [due to antagonisms between the three presidents, who refuse to meet].[29]

This applies particularly to the harbours, railways and some of the airways. As far as the railways are concerned, the system has already broken down, Tanzania having taken the rolling stock from the community for its own Tan-Zam railway; and the rail link to Uganda is bedevilled by border insecurity. Economically, then, the East African Community seems to have little or no future. But politically, at least, the case for keeping up some of the superstructure of the community is strong. There are still, for instance, many Kenyans in Uganda and Tanzanians in Kenya. The most recent (February 1977) development, however, is that in response to several actions by Kenya, such as the grounding of the East African Airways because of non-payment of dues by Tanzania and Uganda, Tanzania has closed its border with Kenya. Kenya has now formally withdrawn from the East African Community, though Tanzania and Uganda still claim to be operating it by themselves.

The problems of achieving any real or permanent measure of success in regional cooperation are very great and emerge clearly from all the examples cited above. What is to be the practical basis upon which to build cooperation between neighbouring states? How can the richer states be protected from the feeling that they are being exploited in order to subsidize their poorer neighbours? Where are the actual development projects to be located? And, perhaps above all, what happens when member states feel that national interests are being overridden by those of the regional groupings? These are questions that have yet to be answered everywhere, and not only in Africa.

African unity

The preoccupation of some writers with the idea of African unity – both on a regional and on a continental scale – is a natural consequence of the rapid devolution of power from European to African hands during the 1960s. In the political flux that has accompanied the transition of Africa from colonialism to independence, several movements for unity have arisen, and they have been both stimulated and sustained by the persistence of white minority governments and colonial regimes in the southern part of the continent. The excessive political fragmentation of Africa has also brought home to its peoples the urgent need for inter-state cooperation. Few African states have sufficient demographic and economic strength to form viable and prosperous political units on their own, and it has already become clear that independence is no guarantee of improved living standards or even of individual political liberties; but grouped together the new states of Africa represent a politically immensely powerful bloc in world affairs.

The phrase 'African unity', however, has many different connotations. One of its meanings is expressed in 'Pan-Africanism', which grew in the 1930s under the inspiration of Americans of African descent. It was never much more than a vague concept – an 'emotion, felt subjectively' – which defied objective analysis, and is now of little significance. It has certainly passed its heyday, based as it was essentially on anti-colonial sentiments; but it did provide the philosophical framework for such ideas as a 'United States of Africa', an 'African Federation', and a 'Union Government of Africa'. In the 1930s, too, the idea of 'Négritude' was born 'out of the revolt of African culture against the French policy of cultural assimilation'. Senghor, the originator of Négritude, has spoken of it as 'the whole complex of civilized values – cultural, economic, social and political – which characterize the black peoples, or, more precisely, the Negro-African world . . . The sense of communion, the gift of myth-making, the gift of rhythm, such are the essential elements of Négritude'. Yet another vaguely defined but emotive concept is that of the 'African personality', with its combination of self-assertiveness and sense of an underlying continental unity.

All of these expressions are similar in being conceptual notions of, rather than practical programmes for, African unity; all are based on the idea that Africans have 'something in common'; and all have developed out of a desire to give positive meaning to African independence. But as yet they have made little impact on practical cooperation between African states, and what little political unity has developed seems to be an expression of combined opposition to vestigial colonialism or to neo-colonialism, rather than the result of a positive desire for African unity as such. The OAU was set up in 1963 with the aim of integrating African opinion and forging common policies of political and economic action. It has so far met with little success, but this provides no justification as yet for dismissing it as a potentially effective instrument for fostering one form or another of African unity.

The positive motives underlying attempts to bring about African unity fall into two main though not mutually exclusive categories. First, there is the desire to reduce the excessive political fragmentation and national parochialism of African states and to eliminate friction between them. Armah, for instance, argues that following the replacement of colonialism by nationalism there should be a United Government of Africa, for in no other way can he see an end to past political struggles and the beginnings of effective collaboration.[30] Secondly, there is the wish to achieve economic advance, it being argued that economic development in Africa can come only from cooperation and coordination between states, and not from fostering the growth of autarchic national economies.

This distinction is important because it bears on the two contrasted ways commonly envisaged for the achievement of African unity, whether at the regional or Pan-African levels. One is the rapid and wholesale political approach, in which national sovereignty is subordinated to the needs of unity, from which it is expected that economic and social cooperation will ultimately flow. The other approach is that which encourages economic and social cooperation in the belief that this alone can form a realistic basis for eventual political unity. In the late 1950s and early 1960s, these different viewpoints were expressed through two groupings: the Casablanca bloc, which supported a sweeping political approach; and the Monrovia group, which supported a gradualist, economic approach. Neither approach, however, has resulted in any considerable measure of unity.

The foregoing chapters of this book have indicated some of the practical difficulties that stand in the way of African unity. The great size and political fragmentation of the continent; the relatively small population; the forces of ethnicity and élitism; the differing past and present associations with European powers of the new African states, with all the economic, cultural, educational and linguistic differences these imply; the continuance of white-minority regimes in southern Africa; and the uneven pattern and widely differing levels of economic activity: all these factors make African unity peculiarly difficult to achieve. Furthermore, the fundamental division of African countries into those lying to the north and south of the Sahara is already expressing itself in a number of new ways. It is true that since the oil crisis African states have been at pains to strengthen Afro-Arab relations both within the continent and outside. But each Pan-African meeting appears to widen the cleavage between northern Africa – Arab, Moslem and increasingly part of the Arab League Community of the Middle East – and Africa south of the Sahara, where the dominant unifying force is Négritude and from which the Arab north is necessarily excluded. This remains almost as true even for those parts of Africa south of the Sahara where Islamization is proceeding most rapidly.

It is in fact pertinent to ask whether the goal of African unity is really either desirable in theory or attainable in practice. The view of black Africa's most powerful nation – Nigeria – is highly relevant here. Because of the difficulty she has experienced in uniting the disparate groups within her own borders, she is sceptical of the practicability of a supranational state in Africa. Nigeria regards Pan-Africanism as a political utopia rather than as a realistic goal. Moreover, it is surprising that there should be so much talk of unity in Africa when, after all, little attention is paid to the prospects of Asian or Latin American unity. Much of the contemporary interest in African unity may be only an extension of the illusion, mentioned in the introduction to this book, that Africa is a continent with a fair degree of homogeneity. But if, as concluded earlier, there is no justification for assuming that it is markedly more uniform than other continents, then it is difficult to argue that there is today any compelling basis for African unity. An examination of the OAU Charter illustrates how national integrity has been protected to the extent of making it impossible for the OAU to take effective action in solving Africa's most pressing problems, even though it has certainly played a useful conciliatory role in some conflicts. Seen in the long perspective of African history, the transition of most of the continent from colonial status to independence has taken place with extraordinary speed. Is it reasonable to expect African nations easily or voluntarily to give up the realities – even the harsh realities – of their new-found independence for the uncertainties of a vague and hypothetical African unity of the future?

8 Africa and the world

Until the early 1970s world interest in Africa remained for the most part peripheral, and it is important to be clear about the reasons for the sudden and dramatic growth of interest over the last few years. At least four main reasons may be identified. First, as indicated earlier, the large number of independent states in Africa – almost one-third of the total membership of the United Nations General Assembly – means that, taken together, they constitute the most important single bloc, even though many of the individual states appear to be insignificant and weak. Secondly, the world is concerned with Africa as a storehouse of important, including strategic, minerals – oil, uranium, chrome, nickel, copper, gold and diamonds – and basic agricultural commodities, notably palm oil, groundnuts, cocoa, cotton, sisal, tobacco and coffee, as well as hides and skins. As a source of economic wealth, indeed, Africa is now probably even more important to the outside world than it was in colonial times, and western investment in Africa is very substantial. Thirdly, the strategic importance of Africa – to the Mediterranean world, the Middle East, the Indian Ocean and the South Atlantic – is only too apparent.

But the fourth reason – itself closely related to the first three – is perhaps of greatest importance in accounting for the current world preoccupation, even obsession, with African affairs. This is that Africa, the most colonized and the last to be de-colonized of all the continents, seems to be experiencing neo-colonialism and, related to this, is increasingly being thought of as a major arena for the conflicting ambitions and ideologies of the western and communist worlds.

Neo-colonialism

In most countries in Africa today it is difficult to avoid the impression that the continent is as fertile a field for the conflicting commercial and investment ambitions of non-African powers as it was for the conflicting territorial ambitions of European countries during the scramble for Africa in the late nineteenth century. On all sides the competition for industrial, agricultural and infrastructural contracts of all kinds is intense, and the capitals of almost all countries seem to be flooded with potential investors and businessmen, with every kind of international agency, and with innumerable experts from many parts of the world. All this is in addition to the continued dependency of most African countries on the developed industrial world as markets for their primary commodities – as destinations for the products of their export-based or 'colonial' economies. As Nkrumah argued, an independent nation is neo-colonial if 'its economic system and thus its political policy is directed from outside'.

Before rushing to the simplistic conclusion that this neo-colonialism is as inimical to the interests of independent African nations as was the earlier period of European colonial control, however, it is important to recognize that part, at least, of the interest and involvement in Africa on the part of the outside world reflects the legitimate concern of international, and especially United Nations, agencies in the social and economic development of Africa as among the poorest regions of the Third World. The current anti-onchocerciasis (river blindness) campaign in West Africa, for instance, organized under the auspices of the World Health Organization, is one example of this legitimate and laudable kind of help from outside. Here, in the seven countries along the Volta river basin (Ivory Coast, Upper Volta, Mali, Ghana, Togo, Niger and Benin) it is planned to wipe out the vector – the *Simulium* sandfly – over the next twenty years. The Lomé Convention, aimed at improving the trading capacity and opportunities of member countries, could also, presumably, be interpreted in this same altruistic light. A similar comment might be made about the protocol of cultural cooperation between Togo and the USSR which provides a Chair of Russian at the University of Benin and scholarships for Togolese: presumably no western observer would complain of a similar agreement being made between, say, Nigeria and Britain. It is not even as if the recipient countries confine their agreements to countries of one ideological bloc. In Togo, apart from the agreement with Russia just mentioned, a new agreement was negotiated with France in 1976 dealing mainly with cooperation in economic and technical spheres, cultural affairs, scientific research and military technology. French investment in Togo's industry includes the building of a phosphate fertilizer plant and a sugar refinery. Five training aircraft and two coastal patrol vessels (the total naval force of Togo) have also been donated.

Part of the problem of external involvement is a matter of styles – of setting standards and values which, however desirable in themselves, may be restrictive on indigenous initiative and subsequent development. Such an argument has been made against the existence of international agencies or research institutes whose motives it is impossible to suspect. An example of this is the work carried out in several such institutes into higher yielding cassava and other basic foodstuffs, but where the whole lifestyle, atmosphere and standards are so far removed from their African context that the institutes can be said to be inhibiting indigenous work; furthermore they are said to be necessarily more concerned with the process of outwards diffusion rather than with the much more difficult problem of the acceptance of innovations. Even where the interests of an agency, country or firm are quite clearly based on self-interest – the capturing of a road-building project for instance – this is presumably no less legitimate in Africa than in any other part of the world where host governments actively encourage competitive bidding for such contracts.

Then there is the whole area of aid and trade, including the activities of UNCTAD. This is a highly controversial issue which we cannot go into here except to point out that to some writers all aid and trade is a form of imperialism or neo-colonialism: most aid and trade assistance simply maintains dependency and reduces the incentive for self-help or self-reliance. The difficulty, of course, is that any interest or involvement in the social and economic betterment of an African country by a non-African state is always likely to be interperted as having sinister underlying political motives; much western comment on Soviet, Chinese or Cuban activity in Africa is of this kind, as is a great deal of Russian comment on western involvement and investment. It must also be recognized that neo-colonialism is not entirely, in some countries is not even largely, a matter of purely external involvement. Neo-colonialism may come from within, especially from African élite groups. In Nigeria, for instance, there are some 70,000 expatriates in the country; but there is a much greater number of Nigerian 'new élites' who act together with the expatriates to confirm and perpetuate neo-colonialism.

The west and communism in Africa

The concern in the west over what is termed the 'communist threat' in Africa is becoming intense. As a former British prime minister, Lord Home, put it:

> there is [in Africa] one large power that is ready to stir the pot of trouble. The USSR is arming Libya as a threat to Egypt; it is also sending arms and equipment into Algeria

with a view to making things hot for Morocco. There is a government in Nigeria that is infected with communism, and in command of a well-trained army. The Soviet Union has used Cubans to take advantage of civil strife in Angola, and is helping Mozambique to organize trouble for Rhodesia.[31]

How far this concern is justified by the facts remains to be seen and is a matter of opinion. Events in Mozambique and Angola, and more particularly the success of left-wing guerrilla armies in taking over these two countries has, perhaps, pinpointed the problem for most observers. In Angola, more especially, the victorious group was not only Marxist in its ideology; the MPLA was also strongly backed by Russia whereas the defeated FNLA and UNITA forces were supported by South Africa, Zaïre and, more covertly, by China and the United States. In the Angolan war, moreover, Russian money, transport, materials and above all weapons were used and the Russian-backed Cuban forces, transported to Angola by Russian planes, were largely responsible for the military successes of the MPLA on the ground. At the same time, due partly to the legacy of defeat in Vietnam, Watergate and revelations about the CIA in the United States, and partly to the backing for the FNLA in South Africa, the United States was obliged to withdraw its support. To the outside world, then, the Angolan affair highlighted, perhaps exaggerated, the potential confrontation between the communist and western worlds; the strength and decisiveness of Russian action was contrasted with the indecision and lack of political will on the part of the western powers. At about the same time, too, revelations about the relative strengths of the Warsaw Pact and NATO countries in any potential conventional armed conflict in Europe encouraged the fear of east–west confrontation. The geopolitical implications of further Cuban and Russian-backed armed conflict in southern Africa, spurred on by what appears to be the final and inevitable conflict between whites and blacks in Rhodesia and South Africa, are widely believed to be serious. The whole of southern Africa, so it is argued, could swiftly become part of a new Russian empire. The theory which the

Russians are following in their relations with Rhodesia and South-West Africa, more particularly, is that only armed struggle, not diplomacy, will win the day for the Africans; that a long armed struggle is the surest route by which revolutionary parties can come out on top.

Certainly many of the facts can be interpreted to support this view. Until recently, it was argued that the main elements of Soviet strategy show Tanzania, Uganda (where Russia is the main arms supplier) and Ethiopia already within the Russian orbit, together with the former Portuguese colonies of Angola and Mozambique – 'the first fully Marxist state in Africa'. Apart from providing the Soviet Union with valuable port facilities along the African seaboard from Mogadishu on the Indian Ocean coast to Lobito in the South Atlantic, this provides a solid basis for the encirclement of South Africa. It is not difficult, continues the argument, to identify the next immediate targets as Rhodesia and South-West Africa. Whatever may be the eventual outcome of the Geneva Conference on Rhodesia, Soviet policy is directed towards the establishment of a Marxist–Leninist Zimbabwe. In South-West Africa the aims are similar, and should Soviet plans succeed in both Rhodesia and South-West Africa then the political encirclement of South Africa will be complete. Whatever one might say about the internal policies of the South African government, South Africa is crucial to the security of the west. According to Lord Chalfont, no one, 'even the most myopic or self-deluded, can be in any doubt that if the mineral resources of southern Africa or the oil routes around the Cape can be effectively denied to the west, the global balance of military and economic power will have undergone a fundamental and dangerous shift'.[32]

Elsewhere in Africa, too, the same kinds of facts can be used to argue the same case. In West Africa, Guinea Bissau has a Marxist government (PAIGC), as do São Tomé and Principe (MLSTP); and the new government of Benin (formerly Dahomey) is avowedly a 'Marxist–Leninist' government. There the ruling party (the Benin People's Revolutionary Party) has changed the name of the country from Dahomey to

Benin 'because the name Dahomey is a colonial one', and the government now 'has its roots in the country's working class, poor and middle class peasantry, and manual workers. It calls on party intellectuals to spread Marxist–Leninist revolutionary ideology'. Guinea, Mali and Nigeria also have strong links with the Soviet Union, as do the Congo, the anti-Mobutu faction in Zaïre, noted in an earlier chapter, Equatorial Guinea, Algeria and Libya. There are also major Soviet economic projects – in Malagasy, the Central African Empire and Ghana, as well as in the countries already mentioned. Again, Cuban military missions are active in many places, including Ethiopia, the Congo, Cameroon and Gabon. Another point is sometimes made that the Arab world, largely outside Africa and largely anti-western if not actually pro-Russian, is increasingly identifying itself with Africa, including of course the North African states; and a union of 21 members of the Arab League and all 47 members of the OAU is now being created. Finally, the new accord between Russia and Libya, expressed in many Russian economic projects in Libya, may well result in Russia being given use of Libyan military bases, giving the Soviet Mediterranean fleet and its air support squadrons splendid harbour and airfield facilities – something Russia has wanted badly since Egypt broke off its relations with Moscow over two years ago. It would also provide Russia with access to Libya's rich oil fields.

In trying to understand the 'communist threat' in Africa it is wrong to think of it simply in ideological terms. Many Africans would emphasize rather the practical and positive social and economic benefits it brings. Moreover, it is important to recognize that Russia's most successful 'intervention' in Angola was in fact carried out by Cuba, a country presenting recognizable parallels for Africans in terms of its struggle against American imperialism and its own poverty; the same could be said of China. In this sense the appeal of communism to Africa is wholly understandable. African nations may be attracted by the anti-colonial and anti-imperialist assumptions of the socialist and communist countries, but they are even more impressed by the practical examples of the Soviet, Chinese and Cuban advance in their agriculture, industries and social services. They are impressed, too, by the ostensibly non-élitist philosophy and absolute racial equality they preach. The dependency theory of development – that underdevelopment is the result of dependency on the industrial world – is currently gaining ground very rapidly. It is recognized, however, that without revolution African countries are not going to extricate themselves from this stranglehold, for it is against the interests of the African bourgeoisie, and of existing governments largely composed of members of this bourgeoisie, to disengage on any effective scale; moreover international capitalism will always make sure that African governments stay afloat by granting aid where necessary.

To many western observers, then, the danger of the Soviet communist presence in Africa is real and serious, and it is feared that any rift between the west and communism will express itself in a confrontation of some kind on the African continent. Indeed, the movement of Soviet communism into Africa can be interpreted as a further chapter in the inexorable drive of Russia for world domination. As we noted in an earlier chapter, the western democratic forms of government left to African independent governments are now largely destroyed. Liberation movements have so often been succeeded by totalitarian governments, or by governments tied irrevocably in one way or another to one or other of the great world powers. From outside come two attacks – the communist and the anticolonial – working simultaneously, and the communist states are working hard to make them a fully combined operation, notably in southern Africa. If successful, this would set most of Africa to join some three-quarters of the world's peoples against the west. The implications of this, not only for the west but also for Africa, are surely unacceptable. The new nations of Africa have appallingly difficult problems of their own to solve, and they must avoid being the arena for any conflict between the communist and western worlds.

On the other hand, this kind of interpretation and analysis is certainly open to question, and by many observers is dismissed as nothing less than egregious nonsense. The danger of any Soviet or communist hegemony in Africa is said to be grossly exaggerated. It is pointed out that the Soviet and other communist countries have had contacts with Africa reaching back at least to the early 1960s on some considerable scale, usually with little success. Russia began in the 1960s by trying to gain substantial influence on both sides of the Red Sea. It was successful in getting military facilities in Somalia but it had its setbacks in Sudan, with the abortive communist-led coup in 1971, and in Egypt, where relations have deteriorated with Russia since 1972. In the 1960s, too, Russia made determined efforts in Zaïre, Ghana, Guinea and Mali, but only in Guinea did she gain any significant success. By the end of 1977, in fact, Russia could be said to have made remarkably little headway in Africa, being forced to make an ignominious withdrawal even from Somalia.

Indeed, it could be argued that Africans are ethnic and nationalistic in their loyalties rather than ideological or interested in international communism; and that the fiercely independent nature of Africans makes the general imposition of any Soviet imperialism as certain to fail as western colonialism failed. To some observers the simple fact that Africa is so vast and diverse a continent means that it is as unlikely to be successfully governed from Moscow, Peking or Havana as it was found impossible to do from European capitals during the colonial period. Again, how, it is asked, can 'proletarian internationalism' be relevant in a continent where there is as yet virtually no proletariat?

Whatever the merits of these opposing lines of argument, there is little doubt that there is a tendency to lump the USSR, Cuba and China together in a way that is both inaccurate and misleading. Many of the arguments emphasizing the communist threat in Africa seem to apply only to Soviet and Cuban interest and involvement and very little to that of the People's Republic of China. If there is any widespread or potentially widespread interest in an ideology in Africa it is more Chinese than Russian in its inspiration. It is the Chinese model – not the Russian model – that is now more frequently cited as the most attractive and practical for African governments to follow.

Within Africa it is the Tanzanian experiment, based as it is so closely on the Chinese model, that attracts greatest interest, and very many countries in Africa now have Chinese groups working, for instance, on agricultural demonstration farms. To the western world the Chinese presence in Africa is perhaps only a 'threat' in the sense that it bids fair to be more successful in social and economic as well as political terms than western capitalism. But China's real short-term aim is certainly to increase her influence in Africa as a means of reducing Russia's role in the Third World. As yet nowhere in Africa is there any indication of a general and solid acceptance of any particular form of socialist or communist ideology on the part of the bulk of the population. Even in Angola the MPLA represents but one section of African opinion; there is a clash of ideologies within the MPLA between those who favour an absolute state-directed economy and those who want a moderate, African socialist state with room for private, including western, capital. Moreover, a substantial body of UNITA guerrillas still operates against the MPLA in Angola. The so-called 'communist' threat in Africa is probably no less complex and diffuse than is the so-called 'western imperialist' threat. Nigeria is a case in point. While one can easily identify the Soviet or communist influence in Nigeria, one can equally point to western 'imperialist' influence; and Nigeria's official position regarding the power blocs of the world is, like so many other countries in Africa, one of non-alignment.

This point can be taken still further. As Legum has recently pointed out, Sino-Soviet rivalry in Africa is perhaps more active and real than any communist-western rivalry; and this fact clearly holds both perils and opportunities for the west.[33] Apart from the Angolan case, the Chinese have generally become more acceptable to African governments than have the Russians. In this sense the Chinese 'threat' is vastly greater than the Soviet 'threat'. The Chinese were quick to adapt their methods to the response of Africans.

Avoiding blatant bids for political domination, and tailoring their programmes to meet the particular requests of the

Africans themselves, they imparted a sense of both generosity and disinterest in their aid role which has led to their steadily widening sphere of friendly influence on the African continent . . .

Their aid is given in an unpatronizing and low-key style. This was true even of their building of the Tanzanian 'freedom' railway (the Tan-Zam railway), and China is at present negotiating to take over the section of the Rhodesian railway in Botswana. Moreoever, most of the liberation movements in southern Africa – notably FRELIMO, ZANU and SWAPO – seem to be working bettter with the Chinese than with the Russians. In Angola, however, the Russians gained complete initial success, and it cannot but be admitted that for a time the outcome of the Angolan affair shifted the balance of influence between the Soviets and Chinese in Africa more to the advantage of Russia. The Soviet Union demonstrated its willingness and capability to produce effective military support for an ally in a strategically crucial part of Africa. In so doing, the Russians succeeded in encouraging other liberation movements to think seriously about accepting their support. Yet one certain thing is the Chinese determination to ensure that the Russians do not repeat their Russian/Cuban/MPLA victory in Rhodesia and South-West Africa.

This conflict between Russia and China in Africa provides the west with some opportunity, at least, for playing a more effective role in southern Africa than if they were confronting a united communist threat. And only if the Sino-Soviet rivalry for influence in Africa 'is given the emphasis it deserves can one understand the true nature of the struggle that is now taking place in Rhodesia and, prospectively, in South-West Africa and South Africa'.[34] The west must realize that African leaders at the moment see white racialism as a greater immediate threat than any form of communism, and that while the United States, for instance, seems willing to support South Africa's plan for independence in South-West Africa without the full participation of SWAPO, then African governments have little choice but to accept backing from the communist worlds. Western powers should also note that there is some hope in the line taken by the so-called 'front-line' presidents (of Tanzania, Mozambique, Zambia, Botswana and Angola) to control what they see as the inevitable war in Rhodesia, and more particularly to avoid it being used, as Angola was, as a battlefield for the conflicting ambitions of the big powers. Their policy is not only to keep the war short and confine it to Rhodesia, but also to channel *all* aid or foreign assistance, military or otherwise, through the OAU's Liberation Committee at Dar es Salaam, to allow fighting only by Zimbabweans, and to ban any new foreign military instructors from being admitted to the training camps for the war in Rhodesia.

Whether events will allow such moderate policies to prevail is very doubtful. Yet such policies demonstrate that African governments are at least fully aware of the dangers of allowing themselves to be drawn into the contest between the west, China and Russia in Africa, and that African leaders would prefer to keep at least this particularly virulent form of neo-colonialism at bay. Whether they will be able to do so, however, is very questionable; it must depend to a large extent on how soon or in what way the Rhodesian problem is solved.

It is clearly in southern Africa that the attention of the outside world is now focused, but it is also in the Horn of Africa that the interests of the west, China and Russia may soon overlap and cause increasing tension. Perhaps the greatest immediate threat to NATO powers comes from Russia's activities in the Horn of Africa, and from her attempts to increase her influence over the whole region and, more positively, along both sides of the Red Sea. The spark setting off a more serious upheaval here may be the territory of the Afars and Issas (Djibouti), which became independent from France in 1977. While only small (less than 9,000 square miles) and largely semi-desert, its value lies in its command of the southern entrance to the Red Sea and Suez Canal, and in its position on the sea route to France's remaining possession (Réunion) in the southern Indian Ocean. The 1973 upheaval, the Soviet presence in Somalia, the revolution in Ethiopia (together with its Eritrean problem), and the opening of the Suez Canal, have given Djibouti fresh strategic significance. The port of Djibouti remains Ethiopia's major life-line, whatever happens in Eritrea. However, in the Afars and Issas, the two major ethnic groups lean respectively towards Ethiopia and Somalia; but the latter are in the majority and will doubtless attempt to cede the territory to Somalia. What will the west do to counter these various pressures? Has the west, as so many observers claim, no deep-rooted strategy at all for countering communism in Africa? Rather than having any strategy for combating communism in Africa, the west appears to be pushing African countries into the arms of Russia and China by failing to appreciate the pace of political change in southern Africa; by its well-meaning but obviously impotent influence on the realities of the situation in Rhodesia, South Africa and Namibia; and by being quite unable to provide any appropriate ideology or strategy for African development.

It is perhaps inevitable that this chapter should have focused so much on the interests of the outside world in Africa, and it is worth emphasizing once again the remarkably recent development of this concern. The 'dark continent' is now the continent of opportunity. Its economic and political, yet alone strategic, value is potentially enormous. And yet it would be to misunderstand the relationship of Africa with the outside world if one were to leave it at that. What of Africa's view of the world? From within, Africa has an ambivalent view of those parts of the world – notably the west, Russia, China and Japan – which are bidding for its favours as strenuously as did the Europeans to exploit them in the past. To this extent African states are suspicious and reluctant to commit themselves to any one state or group of states in the outside world. As we have already noted, links exist between Muslim Africa and the rest of the Arab world; and this may become a factor of increasing importance in the future, though the paucity of Arab funds being invested in Africa generally and in Muslim Africa in particular is remarkable. Then again, many African states are members of the British Commonwealth, and to varying extents feel themselves part of this wider world grouping. The same can be said of African associated membership of the EEC. And yet, on the other hand, Africans envy and generally wish to emulate the technological achievements of the west; and the west is acutely aware that the only effective counter to communism in Africa, as elsewhere, is economic prosperity and stability. Africans are also aware of how far they still have to go in material progress as well as in social and political organization; they are fully aware of their own weaknesses and vulnerability; and they know that they must somehow retain their own freedom of action while making the difficult choices facing them in the period of necessarily rapid change which now confronts them.

Conclusions

The global context of much of the final chapter was no doubt legitimate and important, and it represents the scale at which the outside world tends to regard Africa and its affairs. But in some ways it also represents what is essentially a rather speculative, abstract and academic analysis of Africa and its most immediate problems. To this extent is leaves one rather out of touch with the reality of African affairs as most Africans see them. The world view may be as misleading as is trying to generalize about Africa and its problems from an acquaintance, however long or deep, with one village or even ethnic community. The global geopolitical and social anthropological viewpoints have at least this in common.

The most appropriate scale at which to approach African affairs today must of course depend on the precise issue under scrutiny, and it may well be that several scales need to be adopted simultaneously. In discussing apartheid in South Africa, for instance, the internal considerations are incomplete without reference to the effect of apartheid on views and actions in other parts of southern Africa, on Africa as a whole, and on United Nations interests and global strategy. This is impossible to deny. On the other hand, issues like the creation of an effective sense of national unity in Nigeria or Tanzania are too often made examples of a particular set of hypotheses or theories postulated by political scientists. Yet the universal qualities of, for instance, the study of nationalism in Nigeria or Tanzania are so much less, or at least are so much less interesting, than their differences. Each case represents a largely unique blend of factors which alone can provide a valid background for even the beginning of understanding. To put it another way, most of the current issues in African affairs can best be understood and analysed at the level of the nation state, and not at the level of the African continent, international relations or some other particular social science discipline. However one might try to generalize about 'African affairs' it must be emphasized that there is probably no single identifiable 'African' problem with one 'right' solution. Nigeria's problems are very different from those of Tanzania and so, presumably, require different solutions.

One's perspective of African affairs is also suspect to the extent that it is a European, or at least a non-African, perspective; and this is a point worth making if only because the patronizing tone of so many commentators makes it clear that there is no general recognition of what should be a truism. It is, to put it bluntly, impossible for any non-African ever to be sure he fully understands the African's viewpoint, however varied or variable this may be. It is arrogant to pretend otherwise. There is always a certain gap, and no 'introduction' to African affairs can ever take one more than part of the way along the path of understanding. The non-African observer is always in danger of making his analysis intellectual, consistent and logical, rather than emotional and intuitive; furthermore, he is likely to assume that the former is necessarily more valid and penetrating than the latter. Yet, as Senghor has put it, 'l'émotion est nègre et la raison hellène'. This being so, a European is always likely, however hard he tries, to miss or misinterpret some of the assumptions upon which an African's thought and actions are based.

One of the results of this particular difficulty for non-Africans in their analysis of African affairs is that they become the victims of the myth of objectivity. Just because one describes in detail and with great accuracy an issue in African affairs does not mean that one's comments or conclusions are any more objective or valid than those of someone whose analysis is very much less profound. Thus to describe accurately all the details of the Land Transfer Programme in Kenya, in which land was transferred from whites to blacks, does not mean that one's conclusions or judgements are objective. Even the most cursory acquaintance with commentaries on this particular issue reveals a wide spectrum of conclusions, ranging from 'a brilliantly successful and equitable operation' to 'an act of deep injustice'. It is indeed difficult to exaggerate the importance of this problem of objectivity. There is no such thing as a factual explanation of any event, tempting though it might be to pretend otherwise. To take just two recent examples. The serious riots in Cairo of January 1977 were interpreted variously as having been caused by rising food prices, by a generally deteriorating economic situation, by the growing involvement of western capitalist powers in the Egyptian economy and planning bodies, and by the Soviet Union trying to exploit a relatively small local problem for its own political ends. Clearly all these 'explanations' are related, but the balance of importance between them and their practical implications are a matter of conjecture or opinion, not fact. Similarly, the most recent coup in Ethiopia (1977) was interpreted as having been caused by personal rivalry between the new and former leaders, by ethnic conflicts within the government, and by outside (Soviet) influence. Here again, clear factual explanations are just not possible, and it would be naïve to suggest otherwise. In looking at African affairs where one is enmeshed in a web of conflicting emotions – of race, ideology, colour and even guilt – a non-African faces the problem of trying to retain the capacity to distinguish clearly between fact and opinion, between reality and conjecture.

A second problem for non-Africans in commenting upon African affairs is that, by using their own set of values as the criteria for judgement, they adopt postures which in Africa can only be interpreted as false, mischievous or irrelevant. In this light it is easy to understand, for example, the British government's signal lack of success in influencing Africans and African affairs over the past decade or so. However sincere, concerned and well-meaning the British negotiators may be, to the whites of Rhodesia and South Africa they seem naïve, ill-informed, self-righteous and blatantly hypocritical. To the blacks these same negotiators appear 'colonial' and patronizing, even arrogant, in manner, slow in understanding, and weak and ineffectual in action.

A third characteristic of a non-African's perspective on African affairs is that it is almost always negative and pessimistic. If one is thinking as a European and, however unconsciously, making comparisons with one's own set of values, then such an attitude is understandable. Looking at African affairs from either outside or inside Africa it is impossible to be sanguine about the continent's immediate future; there seems no way in which it can avoid the economic, social and political chaos which seems ultimately certain to engulf it. Africa is certainly ripe for revolution. But this really misses the point. In the complex and continually changing elements of African affairs, it is futile to speculate either too much or too confidently about anything. The understanding, yet alone the solution, of current African problems of the kind we have been looking at in these pages must in the end be reached by Africans themselves. Africans have their own vivid perception of their own problems, as well as their own sets of values and priorities, and in the long run are more likely than anyone else to find practical solutions to them. The danger is not that Africans will be unable to find these solutions but that they will be persuaded or, worse, forced to accept the solutions of others, whether of the west or east. The danger, too, is that African countries will begin to follow the same paths and make the same mistakes as the rest of the world.

If all this is true, it implies that African states must be

allowed to control their own destinies to an extent that external forces now make difficult, if not impossible. The point has already been made on a number of occasions throughout these pages that outside agencies, firms and governments – from the west and from the communist world – are competing vigorously for investment and trading opportunities in Africa; the west and communist worlds are also using Africa as a field for competing ideologies and drawing the continent into the global geopolitical conflict. Events throughout the continent are being manipulated by non-African powers for their own ends. Neocolonialism, dependency and underdevelopment are continuing. On the other hand, it would be naïve to suggest or expect that the rest of the world should agree voluntarily to withdraw from their involvement in Africa. African countries have the right and the responsibility – acting together they also have the power – to make their own choices and decisions affecting their own future. These decisions, choices and initiatives, as well as the interests to be served, must be African – not American, European, Russian, Chinese or Cuban. African states must take what is most relevant and practical from the world outside, adapt it to their own particular set of problems in a manner which is flexible and pragmatic rather than ideological or theoretical, and ensure that they serve, not narrow sectional interests – of party or of ethnic, colour or élite groups – but the interests of the whole population. Clearly there is no universal panacea for any country, let alone for Africa; and each state must make up its own mind about its values, priorities and needs.

Whether all this is mere rhetoric it is up to African governments to decide. But if they do act to make their status as truly independent nations a reality by insisting upon a much greater degree of independence, and by demonstrating a much greater degree of self-reliance and self-confidence than they have so far seemed inclined to do, then there are grounds for optimism about the future of many African countries. There is nothing about Africa or about Africans that makes backwardness, chaos, instability or disorder either necessary or inevitable. The natural and human potential of Africa is immense; but only Africans themselves can realize this potential. If they fail in this, then the peoples of Africa will lose many of the qualities and values of life which they still retain but which are fast disappearing elsewhere. Africa has a great deal to offer the rest of the world and still has time to avoid being caught up in the restless, unthinking drive for material progress and 'development' which is increasingly being shown to be in the interests of few, if any, societies. Indeed, what is there that the rest of the world can really hope to give the peoples of Africa? This is the most difficult question of all to answer. For without in any way idealizing or romanticizing the myriad forms of African society, no one who has lived or worked for long in Africa can doubt that the people who belong to these societies seem to know better than most where human happiness is to be found.

Appendix: *Population of Africa by regions and states, mid-1975*

	Population	Population density per km²
NORTH AFRICA		
Algeria	16,776,000	7
Libya	2,444,000	1
Morocco	17,305,000	39
Tunisia	5,772,000	34
NORTH-EAST AFRICA		
Egypt	37,233,000	37
Ethiopia	27,946,000	22
Djibouti	106,000	5
Somalia	3,170,000	6
Sudan	17,757,000	7
EAST AFRICA		
Kenya	13,339,000	24
Uganda	11,549,000	47
Tanzania	15,155,000	16
WEST AFRICA		
Benin	3,112,000	28
Gambia	524,000	45
Ghana	9,866,000	42
Guinea	4,416,000	18
Guinea-Bissau	525,000	14
Ivory Coast	4,885,000	15
Liberia	1,708,000	15
Mali	5,697,000	4
Mauritania	1,318,000	1
Niger	4,600,000	4
Nigeria	76,700,000	78
Senegal	4,136,000	22
Sierra Leone	2,729,000	38
Togo	2,222,000	40
Upper Volta	6,032,000	22

Population of Africa by regions and states, mid-1975 –
(continued)

	Population	Population density per km²
EQUATORIAL AND CENTRAL AFRICA		
Burundi	3,763,000	135
Cameroon	6,398,000	13
Central African Empire	1,800,000	5
Chad	4,030,000	3
Congo	1,345,000	4
Equatorial Guinea	310,000	11
Gabon	526,000	2
Malawi	5,044,000	43
Rwanda	4,198,000	159
Zaïre	24,902,000	11
Zambia	4,896,000	7
SOUTHERN AFRICA		
Angola	6,600,000	5
Botswana	691,000	1
Lesotho	1,039,000	34
Mozambique	9,239,000	12
Rhodesia (Zimbabwe)	6,420,000	16
South Africa	25,471,000	21
South-West Africa (Namibia)	888,000	1
Swaziland	494,000	28
OTHER TERRITORIES (including small offshore islands)	2,260,000	—
AFRICA TOTAL	407,336,000	14
World Total	3,967,005,000	29

Sources: United Nations, *Demographic Yearbook 1975* (New York 1976), and various country estimates.

References and further
reading

References

1 HERSKOVITS, M. J., *The Human Factor in Changing Africa* (London 1962), p. 14.
2 OLIVER, R. and FAGE, J. D., *A Short History of Africa* (Harmondsworth 1962), pp. 13–14.
3 PERHAM, M., 'The British problem in Africa', *Foreign Affairs*, 30 (1951), p. 132.
4 LUGARD, LORD, 'The white man's task in tropical Africa', *Foreign Affairs*, 3 (1926), p. 14.
5 RYCKMANS, P., 'Belgian colonialism', *in* Quigg, P. W. (ed.), *Africa: A Foreign Affairs Reader* (New York 1964), p. 77.
6 RODNEY, W., *How Europe Underdeveloped Africa* (Dar es Salaam 1972).
7 HARGREAVES, J., *Prelude to the Partition of West Africa* (London 1963), p. 367.
8 NYERERE, J., 'A United States of Africa', *Journal of Modern African Studies*, 1 (1963), p. 5.
9 HERMANS, H. C. L., 'Botswana's options for independent

existence', *in* Cervenka, Z., *Land-Locked Countries of Africa* (Uppsala 1973), p. 197.

10 KHAMA, SERETSE, *quoted in* Hermans, op. cit., p. 211.

11 COHEN, A. (ed.), *Urban Ethnicity* (London 1974), p. ix.

12 ARGYLE, W., *The Dahomey Fon* (Oxford 1965), p. 18.

13 COHEN, A., *Two-Dimensional Man* (Berkeley 1974), pp. 92–8.

14 ibid.

15 LLOYD, P. C., *Africa in Social Change* (Harmondsworth 1970).

16 COHEN, *Two-Dimensional Man*, pp. 99–102.

17 BARRATT, J., 'Southern Africa, a South African view', *Foreign Affairs*, 55 (1976), p. 159.

18 LEGUM, C., 'The Soviet Union, China and the West in Southern Africa', *Foreign Affairs*, 54 (1976), p. 761.

19 *The Times*, 30 November 1976.

20 ibid.

21 SINGER, H. W., Review in *Economic Development and Cultural Change*, 31 (1976), p. 271.

22 PERHAM, M., *The Colonial Reckoning* (London 1963), p. 115.

23 *The Times*, 11 December 1976.

24 *The Daily Times* (Accra), 2 May 1977.

25 MCKINLEY, R. D. and COHAN, A. S., 'Performance and instability in military and non-military regime systems', *The American Political Science Review*, 70 (1976), pp. 850–64.

26 *The Times*, 2 May 1977.

27 LEYS, C., *in* Seers, D. and Joy, L. (eds.), *Developing the Underdeveloped World* (Harmondsworth 1971), p. 8.

28 MILL, J. S., *On Liberty* (Harmondsworth 1976 edn), p. 69.

29 *The Times*, 25 February 1977.

30 ARMAH, K., *Africa's Golden Road* (London 1965).

31 HOME, LORD, 'Africa: time is running out and wisdom is in short supply', *International Perspectives* (July/August 1976), p. 1.

32 CHALFONT, LORD, *The Times*, 22 November 1976.

33 LEGUM, op. cit., p. 759.

34 LEGUM, op. cit., p. 760.

Note: Several passages in chapters 1, 2 and 7 draw on material in Hodder, B. W. and Harris, D. R. (eds.), *Africa in Transition* (London 1967).

Further reading (other than sources cited in the text)

ADAYEMI, S. O., *Nigeria and Africa – A Study of Federal Government Policies, 1966–73*, unpublished PhD thesis (London 1975).

AMIN, G., *Neo-Colonialism in Africa* (Harmondsworth 1973).

ARRIGHI, G. and SAUL, J., *The Political Economy of Africa* (Nairobi 1973).

BOHANNAN, P., *African Outline* (Harmondsworth 1964).

BOHANNAN, P. and DALTON, G. (eds.), *Markets in Africa* (Evanston, Ill. 1962).

BRZEZINSKI, Z., *Africa and the Communist World* (Stanford, Calif. 1963).

CERVENKA, Z., *The Organisation of African Unity and its Charter* (Hurst, Tex. 1969).

CLARKE, J. *et al.* (eds.), *An Advanced Geography of Africa* (London 1975).

COHEN, A., *Custom and Politics in Urban Africa* (London 1971).

DAVIDSON, B., *Which Way Africa?* (Harmondsworth 1971).

DUIGNAN, P. and GANN, L. H. (eds.), *Colonialism in Africa, 1870–1940* (Cambridge 1975).

FAGE, J. D., *Atlas of African History* (Cambridge 1968).

FANON, F., *Toward the African Revolution* (New York 1967).

FORDHAM, P., *The Geography of African Affairs* (Harmondsworth 1974).

GHAI, D. P. (ed.), *Economic Independence in Africa* (Nairobi 1973).

GOODY, J., *Technology, Tradition and the State in Africa* (Cambridge 1971).

GUTKIND, P. and WALLERSTEIN, I. (eds.), *The Political Economy of Contemporary Africa* (London 1977).

HANCE, W. A., *The Geography of Modern Africa* (New York 1975).

HAYTER, T., *Aid as Imperialism* (Harmondsworth 1972).

HAZLEWOOD, A. (ed.), *African Integration and Disintegration* (Oxford 1967).

HILL, P., *Studies in Rural Capitalism in West Africa* (Cambridge 1970).

HODDER, B. W. and UKWU, U. I., *Markets in West Africa* (Ibadan 1969).

LEGUM, C., *Pan Africanism, A Short Political Guide* (London 1967).

LEGUM, C., *Africa Contemporary Record, 1975–6* (London 1976).

LEYS, C., *Underdevelopment in Kenya: The Political Economy of Neo-Colonialism, 1964–71* (Berkeley, Calif. 1974).

LLOYD, P. (ed.), *The New Elites of Tropical Africa* (Oxford 1966).

MAYALL, J., *Africa, the Cold War and After* (London 1971).

MAZURI, A., *Towards a Pax-Africana* (London 1967).

MEILLASSOUX, C. (ed.), *The Development of Indigenous Trade and Markets in West Africa* (Oxford 1971).

NIELSEN, W. A., *The Great Powers and Africa* (London 1969).

NKRUMAH, K., *Neo-Colonialism: The Last Stages of Imperialism* (London 1967).

NYERERE, J., *Freedom and Socialism* (Oxford 1968).

OKIGBO, P., *Africa and the Common Market* (London 1967).

OMINDE, S. and EJIOGU, H., *Population Growth and Economic Development in Africa* (London 1973).

PEIL, M., *Nigerian Politics: The People's View* (Manchester 1972).

WIDSTRAND, C. G. (ed.), *African Boundary Problems* (Uppsala 1969).

Mention must also be made of the numerous valuable papers and journals now devoted to various aspects of the study of Africa. Of particular relevance here are the following: *Africa* (Journal of the International African Institute); *African Affairs* (Journal of the Royal African Society, London); *Africa Research Bulletin* (Exeter); and *West Africa* (London).

Index

economic development planning, 98–100, 122, 129–30
ECOWAS, 125
Edo, 46
education, 17, 22, 24, 51, 53, 58, 62, 68, 92, 95, 103, 122
EEC, 148
Egypt, 6, 23, 31, 100, 114, 138, 143
élite, 16–17, 36, 53–62, 96, 99, 102, 112, 126, 138
élitism, 2, 45, 53–62, 102, 112
Equateur, 104–5
Equatorial and Central Africa, 8, 125–8
Equatorial Guinea, 17, 64, 127, 141
Eritrea, 30, 38, 110
Ethiopia, 10, 19, 23, 30, 38, 110, 146, 151
ethnic group, 6, 32, 34–6, 44–53, 55, 79, 104, 106–7, 110, 113, 115, 122, 125–6, 142
ethnicity, 2, 14, 44–53, 92, 95, 104, 110, 113, 115, 118, 126, 133
Europeans, 3, 6–7, 9–12, 13–26, 54–5, 57–8, 70
Ewe, 32–5, 47, 60, 110
extended family, 51

Fang, 127
Feira, 40
Fezzan, 34
FNLA, 139
Fon, 46–7
France, 12, 16
Freetown, 38, 58, 60
FRELIMO, 73, 145
Fulani, 47, 50
Funj, 9

Gaberone, 113
Gabon, 5, 73, 90, 125
Gambia, 28, 30–1, 36, 91, 101
Ganzankulu, 66
Germany, 12, 32, 52, 78
Ghana (ancient), 9

Ghana, 19, 24, 32, 34–5, 60, 86, 99, 110, 116–17, 120, 123–5, 137
Gisu, 48
Gizenga, 107
Gold Coast, 32
government, types of, 4, 22, 114–19
Great Trek (1836), 65
Guinea, 16, 24, 28, 38, 124, 141
Guinea-Bissau, 140

Hassan, King, 114
Hausa, 9, 32, 47–50, 54, 60–2, 113
health, 22, 95, 104
Horn of Africa, 30, 146–7
Hottentot, 7, 70
Houphöuet-Boigny, F., 51
human resources, 91–2
Hutu, 52–3, 59
hydro-electricity, 21, 31, 90, 109, 122

Ibadan, 6, 48–50, 60–2
Ibo, 45, 47–50, 54, 60, 113
ideology, 4, 82, 94, 110, 141, 143, 147
Igbirra, 46
independence, 2, 23–6, 103, 131
Indian Ocean, 78, 136
Indians, 7, 60, 66, 70–1 (*see also* Asians)
indirect rule, 15–16, 103
industrialization, 57, 69, 91, 109
irredentism, 109–11
Islam, 7–8, 29, 50–1, 61, 133
Ivory Coast, 16, 41, 51, 59, 73, 99–100, 123

Johannesburg, 41

Kakwa, 50
Kalonji, 106
Kampala, 60
Kanem, 9
Kasai, 106, 109
Katanga (Shaba), 31, 103, 105–6, 108

163